A2 Revise PE for Edexcel

A2 UNIT 3

Preparation for Optimum Sports Performance

Dennis Roscoe
Bob Davis
Jan Roscoe

A2 Revise PE for Edexcel
by
Dennis Roscoe
Bob Davis
Jan Roscoe

Jan Roscoe Publications

Published as 978-1-901424-55-3 in 2009 by Jan Roscoe Publications.

'Holyrood'
23 Stockswell Road
Widnes
Cheshire
WA8 4PJ
United Kingdom

tel: 0151 420 4446
fax: 0151 495 2622
e-mail: sales@jroscoe.co.uk

A Catalogue record for this book is available from the British Library

ISBN   Published as 978-1-901424-55-3

Cover designs by Helen Roscoe.

Published via Adobe InDesign, Adobe Illustrator 9.0, Smartdraw 6.0

Printed and bound by

Poplar Services
Poplar House
Jackson Street
St Helens
WA9 3AP

tel: 01744 23363
fax: 01744 451242

www.poplarservices.com

INTRODUCTION

Examination courses in Physical Education have now become established within the post-16 curriculum and are a very popular and successful part of school, college or higher education.

This new edition has been written to address the change in content and style of the Edexcel A2 Physical Education syllabus which commenced in September 2009 (first examination 2010).

This Physical Education course is multidisciplinary in nature, developing a knowledge and understanding of the short-term and long-term physiological and psychological preparations made by elite sportspeople, a little of the history and development of elite sport and the technology of modern sport. These subject areas have generated a substantial quantity of specialist literature each with its own specific language. At times you may be overwhelmed by the amount of material covered in such a one year examination course. 'A2 Revise PE for Edexcel' addresses the problem of dealing with copious notes by summarising the content of the subject matter and attempting to explain in simple language what are sometimes complicated concepts or issues. Practice questions are provided at the end of each chapter, with answers provided on a CD ROM. The answers will amplify the subject matter and provide clues as to how the exam itself should be approached. A new feature this time is the requirement that the final exam questions on each section of the syllabus shall include an essay type answer. This allows students to express their ability and knowledge in the context of properly written language (prose) with attention to grammar and punctuation.

Materials are presented in a concise and visual approach for effective and efficient revision. Modern terminology, nomenclature and units have been used wherever possible. At the end of the book there is a comprehensive index available for easy reference.

Note that the AS course provides the foundation for study of the A2 programme, so students need to refer to "AS Revise PE for Edexcel' ISBN: 978 1 9014242 54 6 for background support.

HOW TO USE THIS REVISION GUIDE

The ideal use of this Revision Guide would be to purchase it at the start of the course and relate each of the summary pages to the specific areas of the syllabus as an aide memoire. The inclusion of specific questions and full answers (see below) provide a means of self-testing. Don't be tempted to find out the answers before attempting a question.

In reality, whole examination questions contain a much broader content than those given in this guide. Examiners will attempt to examine more than one small area of the syllabus within the context of one full question and therefore it is important that you revise all aspects of your syllabus.

The main use of the Revision Guide should be during the final revision period leading up to your examinations, as it should help you to understand and apply concepts i.e. link summary content with examination question.

The aim of this book is to provide an aid that enhances syllabus analysis, and to raise your level of success in examinations.

ANSWERS TO QUESTIONS

The CD ROM enclosed with this book includes answers to all the questions in the text by chapter. You will have noticed that the AS version of this book included the answers in the main text. Feedback from teachers tells us that students have a habit of looking at the answers before actually attempting to derive their own answers as part of the revision process. Hence, people will now have the option of removing or delaying the answers provided by us - to give students a chance to undertake the revision process properly. Note also that although our answers are presented in bullet format, some questions will require to be answered in prose format as mentioned above.

To access the information on the CD ROM, if it does not autorun to bring up a list of chapters, then the main CD directory should be accessed from 'my computer' and the programme 'run.bat' double clicked. This will bring up the list of chapters. Each answer chapter is in pdf format.

THE QUALITY OF AUTHOR

We are an expert team of writers, who have considerable experience in teaching 'A' Level Physical Education, who have written past and current examination syllabuses, who have set and marked examination questions within this subject area and taught at revision workshops throughout the UK. Much of the material within this book has been thoroughly student tested.

We hope that this Revision Guide will prove useful to staff and students. Jan Roscoe Publications will welcome any comments you would wish to make about the book's utility or layout. Thank you for using our work.

Dennis Roscoe
Jan Roscoe

CREDITS

ACKNOWLEDGMENTS

We would like to thank Bob Davis for his co-operation and adherence to our demanding deadlines, and John Norris of Macprodesign for finishing off the graphics and final layouts. We thank Pete Rich for his painstaking proofing of the text. We thank Poplar Services for their patience in linking our work to their computers, and JRP staff member Linda Underwood for working hard in the background while I put this book together. We thank Helen Roscoe for her contribution as cover designer and photographer and the various other graphics authors for the use of their work in this educational context.

Dennis Roscoe
Editor

ACKNOWLEDGMENTS FOR GRAPHICS

Figure 1.21	istock Ludovic Rhodes
Figure 2.16	sport city - Manchester City FC
Figure 2.17	LTA - Wimbledon
Figure 3.3	Steve Parry
Figure 3.7	LTA - Wimbledon
Figure 3.9	Wikimedia Commons/Brett Marlow/Flickr
Figure 3.10	GNU Free Documentation/Wikimedia commons
Figure 3.15	BOA
Figure 3.16	BOA
Figure 3.17	Wikimedia Commons/sonyaandjason/Flickr
Figure 4.9	X-Bionic Clothing
Figure 5.7	istock nikada
Figure 5.9	istock ron summers/damir spanic
Figure 5.23	the stretching institute
Figure 6.6	Wikimedia Commons/Yann Caradec/Flickr
Figure 7.1	Wikimedia Commons/John the scone/Flickr
Figure 7.5	GPSports/Gareth Gilbert
Figure 8.14	GNU Free Documentation/Richard Giles
Figure 8.17	Wikimedia Commons/cfitzart/GNU
Figure 8.18	Mp70 Wikipedia GFDL
Figure 8.19	GNU Free Documentation/Ian Thorpe
Figure 8.26	Wikimedia Commons/White House/Shealagh Craighead
Figure 9.3	Sport Development centre, Loughborough University
Figure 9.4	Sport Development centre, Loughborough University
Figure 9.5	Carnegie Centre for Sport Performance
Figure 9.6	Carnegie Centre for Sport Performance
Figure 9.7	Sport Development centre, Loughborough University

Helen Roscoe is the author of the following graphics:
1.5 / 1.6 / 1.19 / 1.20 / 3.2 / 4.1 / 4.8 / 5.17 / 5.20 / 5.21 / 5.22 / 5.24 / 7.2 / 7.9.

Other photographs/graphics/diagrams are by Jan Roscoe, Dennis Roscoe or Bob Davis.

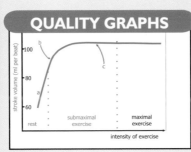

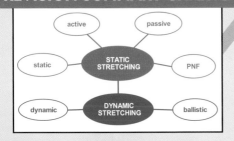
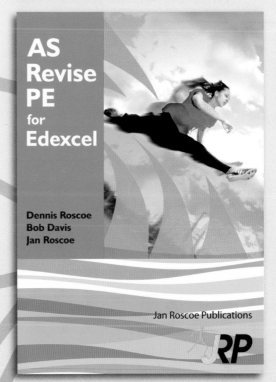

A2 Revise PE for Edexcel

A2 UNIT 3: Preparation for Optimum Sports Performance

SECTION 3.3

MANAGING ELITE PERFORMANCE

SHORT-TERM PREPARATION

CHAPTER 1: *Short-term physiological preparation*

Warm-up

Warm-up is an essential principle of training which **prepares** the body for exercise effort.

Figure 1.1 summarises the issues within warm-up. Warm-up usually consists of a series of **low level aerobic exercises** which can be sport specific or general in nature (jogging, SAQ, cycle ergometer, stretching).

The **sport specific** element usually includes exercises of increasing intensity up to the moment of game or competition beginning.

The **aim** of this element is to get the sportsperson into the **rhythm** and flow of their forthcoming activity, practise skills and movements expected later, and build **confidence** before the event starts.

There are **two** functions of a warm-up, **physiological** and **psychological**, both of which prepare the body for the main exercise effort to come.

Physiological value of warm-up

- Warms muscles and enables better **ATP conversion**.
- Slightly **better blood flow** due to blood viscosity lower at higher temperature.
- Increases the **speed of nerve impulse conduction** and hence faster reaction time.
- Enhances **glycolytic enzyme** action.
- Increase in heart rate and **cardiac output**.
- Increase in **volume of air** breathed per minute (V̇E) thereby increasing availability of oxygen.
- **Capillaries dilate** with oxygenated blood.
- Increase in **blood pressure** forces blood more quickly through arteries.
- Stretching of **relevant joints** and muscle prepares them for full range action.
- Secretion of **adrenaline** increases the metabolic rate (normal rate at which energy is produced by the whole body).
- **Reduces** risk of musculo-skeletal **injuries**.

figure 1.1 – warm-up

Psychological value of warm-up

- Warm-up is a **rehearsal** for skill-related practices (figure 1.2).
- This improves **co-ordination** of the neuromuscular system.
- Warm-up prepares the body psychologically for training or competition by increasing **arousal**. For example, the New Zealand All Blacks perform the Haka (see page 42 below) as part of match warm-up preparations.
- This arousal will heighten awareness of pitch and player positioning and **enable focusing** on relevant aspects of a game.
- This sort of activity builds **self-confidence** or **self-efficacy** for the action to begin.

figure 1.2 – psychological aspects of warm-up

Stretching

Most sportspeople include some stretching in their warm-up routine. However, the inclusion of lengthy stretching in warm-up is controversial, since some research has shown no effect on joint mobility for stretching done during warm-up, and a possible risk of injury if violent static stretches are performed on cold muscle.

But most people use rhythmic stretching movements as part of an effective warm-up programme.

Figure 1.3 outlines the different types of stretching, and page 59 below sets this out in more detail in the context of long-term preparation.

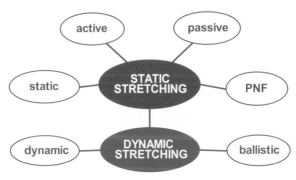

figure 1.3 – flexibility / stretching

STUDENT NOTE

Stretching as a means of improving joint mobility – improving the range of movement at joints as a long-term effect of training - is best performed after or during a session in which muscle has been exercised thoroughly, and is therefore at its warmest.

figure 1.4 – stages of a structured warm-up

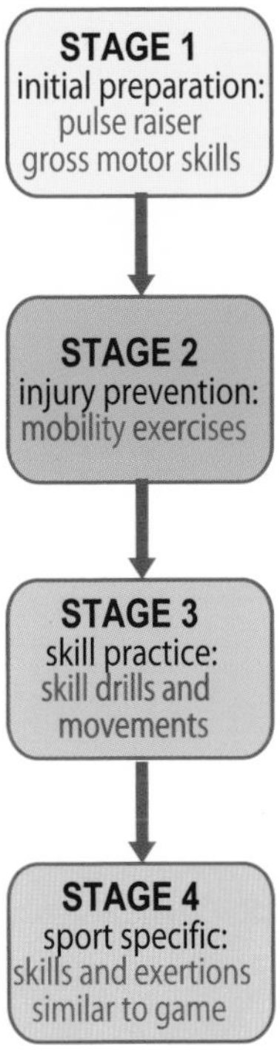

The four stages of a model warm-up

The model outlined in figure 1.4 is used by elite sports teams to enable the physiology and psychology of warm-up to take place in the context of specific movements relevant to the sport itself.

STAGE 1
initial preparation:
pulse raiser
gross motor skills

Stage 1
Gross motor activity involving all major muscle groups (which initiates blood flow to major muscles), for example:
* Jogging.
* Short game or skill-based activity.
* Easy swimming.
* Easy cycling.

STAGE 2
injury prevention:
mobility exercises

Stage 2
Mobility exercises to loosen and relax muscles and joints, which increase localised muscle elasticity. Take care - there is some evidence of injury if these exercises are done too violently on muscle not fully warmed.

STAGE 3
skill practice:
skill drills and movements

Stage 3
Stage 3 includes a **skill-related elemen**t, which works the neuromuscular mechanisms involved in the activity, for example:
* Tennis serves.
* Turns in swimming.
* Delivery drills in throwing.

STAGE 4
sport specific:
skills and exertions similar to game

Stage 4
During this final stage, the sportsperson **practises specific skills**, as the performer would actually experience them in a game or competitive situation.
For example:
* Tennis serves to an opponent, with returns of serve and a response.
* Swimming to the wall, then tumble turn, then swim out to 15 or 20 metres.
* Actually throw from the competitive circle (just prior to competition).

Further structure of a warm-up - intensity and duration

The **intensity** and **duration** of warm-up depend on the demands of the sport or the demands of the training session. Warm-up can vary enormously in both factors. For example:

figure 1.5 – warming up is essential

- An Olympic hurdler and sprinter taking 2 hours (warm-up) for an event lasting less than 10 seconds and incorporating multiple rhythmic and skill-based movements specific to the event.
- The GB hockey team at the Olympics taking 1 hour performing SAQ exercises, moving on to multiple passing and goal shooting plays - all of relatively low intensity.
- An Olympic weightlifter whose competitive effort involves a maximum of 6 efforts each lasting less than 2 seconds. The warm-up involves a systematic build-up for each of the two lifts taking up to 2 hours and involving up to 90% of 1RM practice lifts.
- A rugby team will take 30 minutes with jogging, 80% sprinting and stretching, as well as some high intensity short duration exercises done to the accompaniment of verbal chanting to assist in the psychological preparation.

Sources of energy for exercise

figure 1.6 – all muscle action uses ATP

STUDENT NOTE

Energy for exercise is derived from the food we eat. But first we need to look at the way in which this energy is converted into muscular contractions, which would enable a sportsperson to run, jump or throw, or play games and climb mountains. The notion of nutrition and what is required for a balanced diet have been covered in the AS programme. See page 25 onwards of AS Revise PE for Edexcel, ISBN: 978 1 901424 54 6.

ATP - Adenosine Triphosphate

ATP is the energy currency linked to **intensity** and **duration** of physical activity. ATP exists in every living tissue and its breakdown gives energy for all life functions - this includes the action of the liver and the brain for example, as well as the contraction of muscle tissue.

The energy released during tissue respiration is stored in the chemical bonds in ATP, and this energy is released during the reaction:

$$\text{ATP} \rightarrow \text{ADP} + P_i + \text{energy}$$

where ADP is adenosine diphosphate, and P_i is a free phosphate radical. **ATPase** is an enzyme which facilitates this reaction, which is **exothermic** - it releases energy.

The energy stored within ATP is only available as long as ATP is retained within the cells using it. In muscle cells during intense (flat-out) exercise, the stored ATP only lasts about 2 seconds. Therefore the ATP must be replaced as soon as possible so that exercise can continue. There are **three** processes by which this can happen:

- The **ATP-PC** system (also called the alactic anaerobic system).
- The **lactic acid** system (which is also anaerobic).
- The **aerobic** system.

Resynthesis of ATP from ADP uses the reaction: $\text{energy} + \text{ADP} + P_i \rightarrow \text{ATP}$

This is an **endothermic** reaction since energy is **given** to the molecule to enable the reaction to happen. This energy will be derived from **food fuels**.

The ATP-PC system

This system is the predominant one for activity which lasts between 3 and 10 seconds, which means for high intensity maximum work, for example, flat out sprinting - the 100m sprint.

No oxygen is needed - the process is anaerobic. The chemical reactions within this system are a **coupled reaction** in which ATP is resynthesised via phosphocreatine (PC) stored in muscle cell sarcoplasm.

The following reactions take place: $\quad$ **PC $\rightarrow$ P$_i$ + C + energy**

$$\text{energy + ADP + P}_i \rightarrow \text{ATP}$$

The two reactions together are called a coupled reaction and are facilitated by the enzyme **creatine kinase** (CK).

The net effect of these two coupled reactions is:

$$\text{PC + ADP} \rightarrow \text{ATP + C}$$

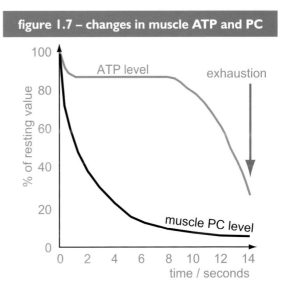

figure 1.7 – changes in muscle ATP and PC

STUDENT NOTE

This process does not directly require glucose as an energy source - but the the recreation of PC during recovery will do so.

PC is recreated in muscle cells during the recovery process, which requires energy and is an **endothermic** reaction.

During intense exercise, peak anaerobic power is attained within the first 5 seconds, and depletion of PC occurs between 7 and 9 seconds.

Look at the graph in figure 1.7 showing changes in muscle ATP and PC. After an initial small fall, the ATP level is maintained, then falls as the PC is used up because the energy from PC is being used to resynthesise ATP. This causes PC levels fall rapidly to zero after about 10 seconds. The capacity to maintain ATP production at this point depends on the lactic acid system.

The lactic acid system

This system depends on a chemical process called **glycolysis** which is the incomplete breakdown of sugar. Figure 1.8 shows the schematic layout of glycolysis.

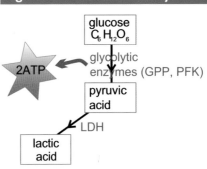

figure 1.8 – the lactic acid system

- Carbohydrate from food you have eaten is stored as **glycogen** (in the muscles and liver).
- This glycogen is converted into glucose by the hormone **glucagon** released when blood glucose levels fall (when glucose is used during tissue respiration).
- The breakdown of glucose provides the energy to rebuild ATP from ADP.
- This is facilitated by enzymes such as **glycogen phosphorylase** (GPP) and **phosphofructokinase** (PFK).
- The whole process produces **pyruvic acid**.
- **Glycolysis is anaerobic**.
- It takes place in the **sarcoplasm** of the muscle cell.
- No oxygen is needed, and the end product of this reaction (in the absence of oxygen) is lactic acid.
- The enzyme facilitating the conversion from pyruvic acid to lactic acid is **lactate dehydrogenase** (LDH).

As work intensity increases lactic acid starts to accumulate above resting values, which produces muscle fatigue and pain. The resultant low pH inhibits enzyme action and cross bridge formation, hence muscle action is inhibited and physical performance deteriorates.

The lactic acid system is the predominant one used to resynthesise ATP in sport or activities in which the flat-out effort lasts up to 30-60 seconds. For example, a 400m run or a 100m swim.

After exercise stops, extra oxygen is taken up to remove lactic acid by changing it back into pyruvic acid - this is the **EPOC** (**Excess Post-exercise Oxygen Consumption** - sometimes called the oxygen debt), see page 44 below for the details of EPOC.

The aerobic system

Figure 1.9 is a graphic showing some of the details of the aerobic system showing how between 32 and 34 ATP molecules are resynthesised from one molecule of glucose - which is the food fuel created from the food we eat. This process will continue indefinitely until energy stores run out - or the exercise stops.

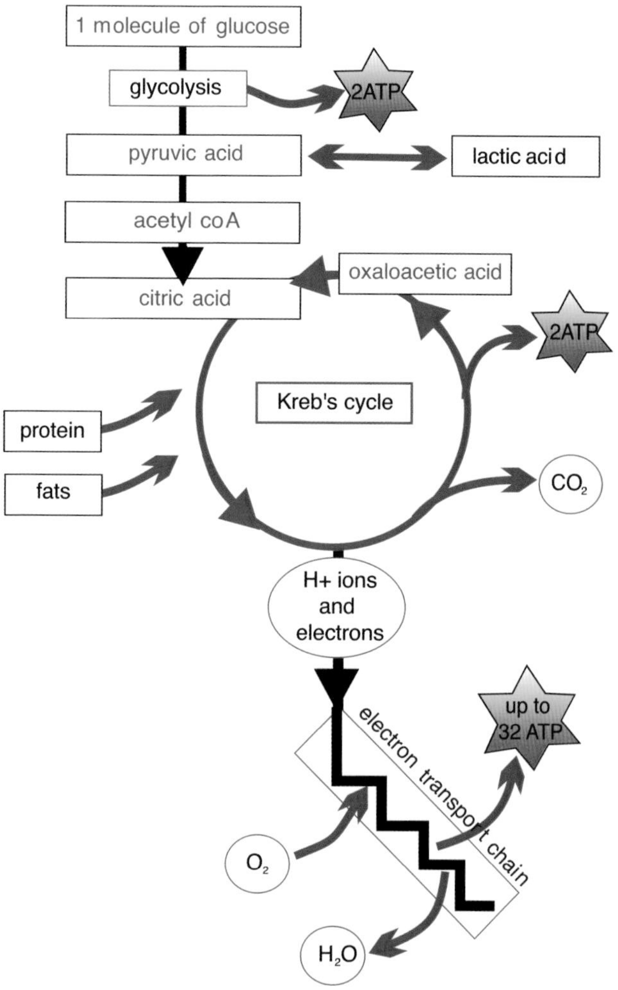

Stage one - glycolysis

This process takes place in the **muscle cell sarcoplasm** and is identical to the lactic acid system (anaerobic).
ATP regenerated = 2ATP per molecule of glucose.

Stage two - Kreb's cycle (citric acid cycle)

This stage occurs in the **presence of oxygen**, and takes place in the **muscle cell mitochondria** within the inner **fluid filled** matrix. Here, 2 molecules of **pyruvic acid** combine with **oxaloacetic acid** (4 carbons) and **acetyl coA** (2 carbons) to form citric acid (6 carbons). The cycle produces H^+ and electron pairs, and CO_2 and 2 ATP. Also, fatty acids (from body fat) facilitated by the enzyme **lipoprotein lipase**, or protein (keto acids - from muscle), act as the fuel for this stage.

Stage three - the electron transport chain

The electron transport chain occurs in the presence of oxygen within the **cristae** (inner part) of the **muscle cell mitochondria**. **Hydrogen ions** and **electrons** have potential energy which is used to produce the ATP which is then released in a controlled step-by-step manner. Oxygen combines with the final H^+ ions to produce water and 32 ATP.

Aerobic respiration

In summary, the total effect of aerobic respiration is that it is an **endothermic** reaction:

$$\text{glucose} + 36 \text{ ADP} + 36 \text{ P}_i + 6O_2 \rightarrow 6CO_2 + 36 \text{ ATP} + 6 H_2O$$

Fat fuels produce 2 ATP less than glucose.

figure 1.9 – the aerobic system

1 molecule of glucose → glycolysis → 2ATP

pyruvic acid ↔ lactic acid

acetyl coA

citric acid ← oxaloacetic acid

Kreb's cycle → 2ATP

protein

fats

CO_2

H+ ions and electrons

electron transport chain → up to 32 ATP

O_2

H_2O

STUDENT NOTE

You should refer to your AS Revise PE for Edexcel page 77 Table 5.1 (ISBN 978 1 901424 54 6) for a summary of ATP regeneration.

Short-term response to aerobic activity

The aerobic system requires carbohydrate in the form of **glucose** which is **derived from glycogen** stored in muscle cells (mostly slow twitch - SO type I) or in the liver.

The graph in figure 1.10 shows how the rate of usage of muscle glycogen is high during the first 30 minutes of steady exercise - which has to be replaced if a sportsperson is to continue at the same rate. Hence consumption of energy drinks and bananas during a long tennis match.

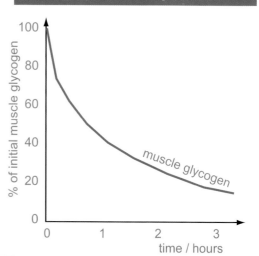

figure 1.10 – change in muscle glycogen during low intensity exercise

% of initial muscle glycogen vs time / hours

muscle glycogen

The energy continuum

This describes the process by which ATP is regenerated via the different energy systems depending on the intensity and duration of exercise. Although **all** the systems contribute to ATP regeneration during any activity, one or other of the energy systems usually provides the major contribution for a given activity. Table 1.1 shows approximate proportions of ATP resynthesised via aerobic and anaerobic pathways for some sporting activities.

Table 1.1 – **percentage contribution of the aerobic and anaerobic energy systems to different sports**

sport or event	aerobic %	anaerobic (all) %
100m sprint	0	100
200m sprint	10	90
100m swim	20	80
boxing	30	70
800m run	40	60
hockey	50	50
2000m rowing	60	40
4000m cycle pursuit	70	30
3000m run	80	20
cross country run	90	10
marathon	100	0

Each of the alactic, lactic acid and aerobic systems contribute some ATP during the performance of all sports.

Other factors affecting the proportions of energy systems

The graph in figure 1.11 shows how the different energy systems contribute resynthesis of ATP during flat-out exercise. Obviously, at reduced intensity of exercise, the contributions will be slightly different. But note that **all systems** are contributing from the start of exercise, only it takes some time for the lactic acid and aerobic systems to get going.

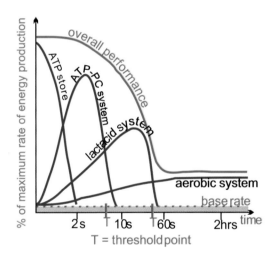

figure 1.11 – variation in contribution of energy system

T = threshold point

The other factors which affect the proportions of contribution are:
* The **level of fitness** (whether adaptations to training have included enhancement of relevant enzymes - which would for example postpone levels of lactate accumulation).
* The **availability of O_2 and food fuels**. For example a high CHO diet would assist replenishment of glycogen stores which would then be available for glycolysis.

Short-term responses - thresholds

The concept of a **threshold** applies to the time at which one particular system of ATP regeneration takes over from another as the major regenerator of ATP during flat out exercise - marked as **T** in figure 1.11.

* For example, **ATP muscle stores** are depleted **within 2 seconds**, and towards the end of this period the ATP-PC system has risen enough to be able to provide the ATP necessary for the exercise.
* **Peak anaerobic power** is attained within the first 5 seconds of flat-out exercise, but depletion of PC occurs between 7 and 9 seconds.
* At this point, the lactic acid system has risen enough to be able to provide the ATP required for the next 40 seconds or so.

Hence the **threshold** between **ATP-PC and lactic acid** systems occurs between 7 and 9 seconds after the start of an exercise period.

Dietary manipulation

A balanced diet

STUDENT NOTE

From the AS course, a balanced diet is summarised in figure 1.12. A balanced diet from a regular food intake will provide the nutrient requirements for all sportspeople. See page 26 of AS Revise PE for Edexcel ISBN: 978 1 901424 54 6.

figure 1.12 – balanced diet

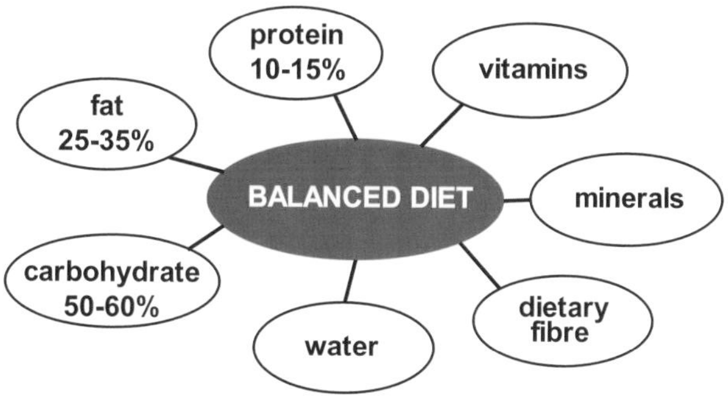

protein 10-15%
fat 25-35%
vitamins
BALANCED DIET
minerals
carbohydrate 50-60%
water
dietary fibre

A high carbohydrate (CHO) diet significantly improves performance. The following **two** elements will start reloading depleted muscle glycogen stores, and ensure enough CHO is available to improve glycogen stores and hence glucose or glycolysis:

- Immediate post-exercise **CHO supplements**.
- **High glycemic index** (GI) foods such as bananas and raisins.

Carboloading (see below) can augment endurance performance in events lasting longer than 90 minutes by increasing muscle glycogen stores above normal levels.
Fat intake should be restricted for both power and endurance athletes except for power events such as sumo wrestling.

Dietary manipulation

This is the notion that sportspeople can change their diet to enhance performance - and this is mostly done via CHO intake.

- **Protein** proportion of diet will change according to the sports activity. For endurance athletes the recommended protein intake is 1.2 to 1.4 grams per kilogram of body mass per day, and since strength and power athletes need additional protein, for them, 1.4 to 1.8 grams per kilogram of body mass per day is recommended. This need for extra protein is because after heavy resistance training the rate of protein breakdown and resynthesis is greater due to muscle hypertrophy.
- Regular intake of **vitamins and minerals** is required for all performers. Research has shown that a normal well-balanced diet provides all necessary vitamins and minerals to support elite performances - although some athletes do take vitamin and mineral supplements to be certain that all these relatively small elements of a diet are covered.
- Dietary **fibre** is also needed at a balanced level and must not be neglected for the elite performer.

figure 1.13 – carboloading

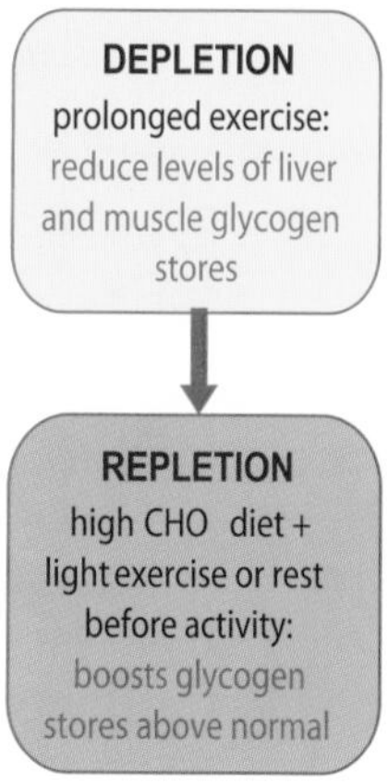

DEPLETION
prolonged exercise:
reduce levels of liver and muscle glycogen stores

↓

REPLETION
high CHO diet +
light exercise or rest before activity:
boosts glycogen stores above normal

Carboloading

Carboloading aims to raise muscle glycogen stores above their normal resting levels prior to endurance competitions with over 90 minutes continuous activity. This process is suitable for activities with low anaerobic and high aerobic components.

Figure 1.13 outlines the **depletion-repletion** model upon which carboloading is based. It is suitable for any activities lasting longer than 15-20 minutes. Note that a two-day high CHO diet beforehand provides the best CHO boost for an endurance event.

Carboloading - glycogen supercompensation

The graph in figure 1.14 shows how the muscle glycogen level returns to above normal values when the depletion-repletion process is undertaken as outlined in the previous paragraph. In effect the body reacts to a loss of glycogen by vigorously replacing it to a level above normal. This is a normal reaction to **biological stress**.

figure 1.14 – glycogen supercompensation

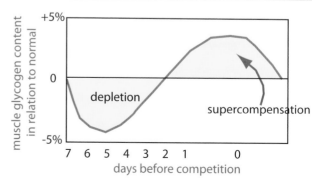

The importance of high glycogen content in muscle before a marathon race

The graph in figure 1.15 shows that a runner's time would increase by around 10 minutes in a 2 hour run if muscle glycogen started at 50% of its maximum possible. The effect of reduced muscle glycogen begins to be felt at the 1 hour mark. Hence the importance of glycogen loading to endurance sportspeople.

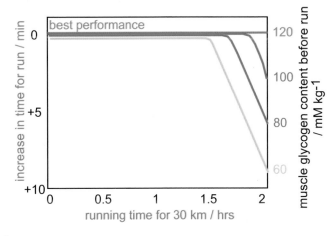

figure 1.15 – effect of glycogen store on endurance running times

Pre-competition nutrition

Should consist of:
• Fluids for hydration.
• Light complex CHO such as pasta or wholemeal bread at least 3 hours before activity.
• Fruit (banana) contains complex CHO.
• Small amounts of glucose.
The effect is to provide the slow release of blood glucose and reduce hunger sensations.

Post-competition or training nutrition

Should consist of:
• **Hypertonic** sports drink immediately after exercise has finished.
• This begins **replenishment of blood glucose** and **glycogen** stores.
• A **high CHO** meal within 15 minutes of exercise ending (or as soon as possible) continues glycogen replenishment.

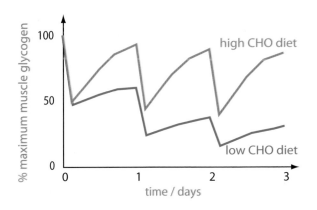

figure 1.16 – the athlete's diet

Nutritional dietary manipulation during training

The graph in figure 1.16 shows the influence of dietary carbohydrate on **muscle glycogen** stores. In this training situation, repeated daily exercise of 2 hours is followed by either a high CHO or low CHO diet.

STUDENT NOTE

Note the difference that high CHO makes to the energy available to the sportsperson, and a major possible reason for exhaustion for those 'on a diet'!

Hydration

Water loss of as little as 2% to 3% can reduce performance, hence an **isotonic sports drink** including very diluted sodium and glucose content, taken during an activity, prevents dehydration and supplements energy reserves. Since water loss has the greater effect, sportspeople are recommended to take in water for any activity lasting more than about 30 minutes.

Body fluid balance
• Water is lost from the body during exercise mainly by sweating from the skin surface.
• The reason that dehydration causes loss of sports performance is because **fluid loss decreases plasma volume** which reduces blood pressure.
• This then causes a **reduction in blood flow** to **skin** and **muscles**.
• Hence the heart has to work harder than it would have to if there were no fluid loss, body temperature rises, and fatigue occurs as aerobic capacity falls (see figure 1.17).
• This is the **cardiovascular drift** - see page 51 in AS Revise PE for Edexcel, ISBN: 978 1 901424 54 6.

Hence **fluid intake is important** during endurance activities.

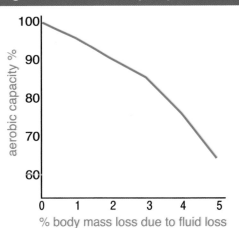

figure 1.17 – aerobic capacity and fluid loss

Fluid loss

- **At rest**, water loss occurs via evaporation and excretion, with the majority lost as urine.
- Water intake depends on climate and body mass.

- **During exercise**, more water is produced during tissue respiration.
- Water is lost mainly as **sweat**, the rate of which is determined by external temperature, body mass and metabolic rate.
- There is increased water loss via **expired air** due to increased ventilation, and the kidneys decrease urine flow in an attempt to decrease dehydration.
- During a marathon, 6-10% of body water content is lost, hence the need for water intake.

During 1 hour's exercise an average person could expect to lose around 1 litre of fluid, and even more in hot conditions which could represent as much as 2 litres an hour in warm and humid conditions.

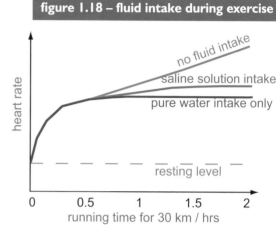

figure 1.18 – fluid intake during exercise

Fluid intake during exercise

As mentioned earlier, water loss of as little as 2% to 3% can reduce performance. The graph in figure 1.18 shows how heart rate is affected by fluid intake during prolonged exercise. Heart rate rise without fluid intake is explained earlier, but the graph also shows how heart rate is kept constant - if suitable water is taken during the exercise.

Creatine supplementation

Creatine is a substance found in skeletal muscle and which is stored as **phosphocreatine** (PC). Creatine supplementation (usually together with large amounts of CHO) increases PC levels to enhance the ATP-PC system of ATP resynthesis, thereby delaying the alactic/lactic threshold. This is a **legal ergogenic aid**.

figure 1.19 – power athletes benefit?

Sportspeople use creatine in a way which will help improve anaerobic power and lengthen the time over which they can apply maximal power. It is not a muscle development 'drug', and eating lots of raw white meat (as in fish) would have the same effect. This is because white muscle cells (those not containing lots of myoglobin, which is red in colour and is present in large quantities in slow twitch muscle cells) are predominantly fast twitch in nature and contain creatine in relatively large quantities.

Power athletes, such as the pole vaulter in figure 1.19, use in their competitive event a little bit of the ATP-PC system and mostly ATP storage. But almost all the training will be serviced by the ATP-PC system, and therefore creatine supplementation will help the training process.

Short-term acclimatisation

Competition or matches in unusual conditions (including changes of time zone) sometimes require time to get used to these conditions. The process of the body getting used to the conditions is called **acclimatisation**. These unusual or different environmental conditions cause the body to adapt because changes occur to its biology.

Periods of time to acclimatise range from a few days to weeks, and the adaptations made by the body as it acclimatises are usually reversible. Hence the adaptations are a short-term response to the change in conditions.

Acclimatisation to high temperatures

To adapt to high temperatures, **blood flow to skin** is increased to enable **greater heat loss** from the skin which can be up to 20 times normal values. **Sweat rate increases**, but this increases dehydration and hence the body adapts by conserving sweat and essential salts. This requires **drinking water continuously** during any physical activity.

As already mentioned in the previous section, **fluid loss decreases plasma volume**, which reduces blood pressure which in turn reduces blood flow to skin and muscles. This forces the heart to work harder than it otherwise would, and forces a rise in body temperature (since the skin cannot radiate out the body's surplus heat energy).

Regulation of body temperature

The **thermoregulatory centre** is situated in the hypothalamus - in the brain. Changes in body temperature are sensed by central and peripheral receptors, and body temperature is maintained by balancing heat input and heat loss. Figure 1.20 lists the heat energy transfer methods from the human body.

Heat input is by:
- Metabolic heat.
- Exercise.
- Shivering.
- Solar radiation.

Heat loss is by:
- Radiation.
- Conduction.
- Convection.
- Evaporation.

figure 1.20 – heat input and output

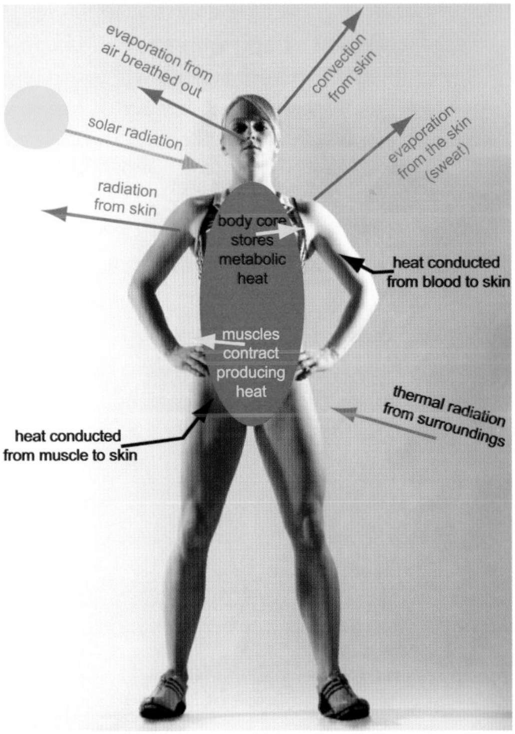

Importance of body fluid balance

The main method by which an exercising body regulates its internal operating temperature in hot conditions is by **evaporation of water** from the skin surface (sweat) and hence fluid loss. Regular intake of fluids will also help reduce the effects of the cardiovascular drift (see page 51 of AS Revise PE for Edexcel, ISBN: 978 1 901424 54 6).

The body also tries to reduce its core temperature by ensuring high blood flow to the peripheral parts of the body (mainly the skin), where the heat stored in the blood is radiated away to the surroundings. This is why a hot and bothered sportsperson will flush (red skin) due to more blood than usual in the facial skin. Common heat-related illnesses include muscle cramps, fainting, and exhaustion.

Table 1.2 – **proportions of the different methods of heat energy transfer from the body**

mechanism of heat loss	% of total at rest	% of total during exercise
conduction & convection	20	15
radiation	60	5
evaporation	20	80

High humidity decreases the capacity to lose heat by evaporation during exercise in hot weather, since it creates competition between the active muscles and the skin for limited blood supply.

The effect of body size
- **Body size** is an important consideration for heat loss. Subjects who have a small **surface area-to-body mass ratio** and more fat are less susceptible to **hypothermia** (cooling to dangerously low levels) but more susceptible to **hyperthermia** (heating up to dangerously high temperatures - heat stroke).
- This is because larger people have bigger heat production in muscle (and other tissue) roughly proportional to their mass. Unfortunately, such people have relatively less skin surface area from which to radiate or sweat away the heat energy.
- Also, people with large amounts of **subcutaneous fat** (under the skin) have a barrier (**insulation**) to heat conduction away from the body core.

- Hence fat (large!) people (figure 1.21) tend to overheat more easily than skinny people.

Short-term adaptations to high temperatures

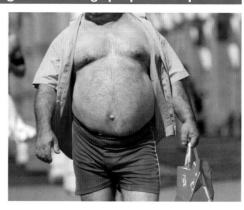

figure 1.21 – large people heat up more?

> **STUDENT NOTE**
>
> Short-term preparation refers to the time immediately before competition. This could be anywhere between several days to hours/minutes prior to the competition.

- In the case of **heat acclimatisation**, repeated exposure to hot environments, when combined with exercise, improves capacity for exercise **with less discomfort** (in hot temperatures).
- Within 3 days there is an increase in plasma volume, thus supporting stroke volume and cardiac output.
- This is combined with the increased ability to sweat, particularly exposed body parts such as arms and legs.
- Sweating leads to a **reduction in core temperature** and therefore a **reduction in heart rate**.
- Therefore more training can be done before the onset of fatigue. This is called heat acclimatisation.

Table 1.3 – **the main physiological adjustment during heat acclimatisation**

figure 1.22 – a pale, cold athlete!

acclimatisation response	effect
improved cutaneous blood flow	transports metabolic heat from deep tissues to the body shell
effective distribution of cardiac output	circulation to skin and muscles to meet demands of metabolism and thermoregulation
	greater stability of blood pressure during exercise
lowered threshold for start of sweating	evaporative cooling begins earlier in exercise
more effective distribution of sweat over skin surface	optimum use of skin surface for evaporative cooling
increased sweat output	maximises evaporative cooling reducing core temperature
lowered sweat salt concentration	dilute sweat preserves electrolytes in the body

- Acclimatisation to **hot**, **humid conditions** results in increased sweating because high humidity contributes little to evaporative sweating.
- Adequate fluid replacement preserves plasma volume to maintain circulation and sweating at optimal levels.
- Full acclimatisation to heat requires about 10 days of heat exposure.
- Women athletes sweat less than men at the same core temperature.

Temperature regulation in cold conditions

In the case of adapting to cold conditions, more heat energy is required to raise the body temperature. This is achieved by repeated muscular contractions - **shivering**, and is accompanied by withdrawal of blood from the peripheral parts of the body (peripheral = away from the core), such as the skin and hands and feet. This is why a person looks pale when seriously cold (figure 1.22).

The fluid thus withdrawn from the skin, hands and feet is then stored in the core, and the kidneys will begin to excrete water as urine to reduce the total fluid volume (plasma volume) held centrally. Hence fluid is lost in cold conditions - and will need to be replaced once the person has warmed up again.

If thick clothing is worn in these conditions, sweating can increase - which would again cause fluid loss and possible dehydration.

Acclimatisation to altitude

The effects of altitude on the respiratory system

The higher the altitude, the more that aerobic performance is affected by the lack of oxygen pressure in the air.

People who live at altitude (for example at over 2000m above sea level) are exposed to air at lower pressure, and hence breathe oxygen at a lower pO_2. Therefore there would be a reduction in pO_2 from 13.3 kPa to 10.2 kPa in alveolar air for such people.

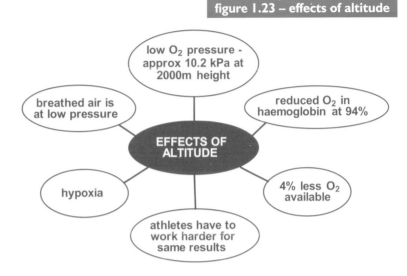

figure 1.23 – effects of altitude

- When you exercise at higher altitudes (see figure 1.23) you will have to work harder to achieve the same sea level performance, because your aerobic system will be taxed that much harder.

- The relative saturation of haemoglobin with oxygen at 10.2 kPa is only 94% (as compared with 98% at pO_2 of 13.3 kPa).
- This is shown in figure 1.24, looking at the vertical dashed blue line. Hence the capability of haemoglobin (Hb) to carry oxygen is reduced by about 4%.
- The lower than normal levels of oxygen in the blood or tissues is known as **hypoxia**.

- This condition would affect the capability of an athlete to perform **aerobic exercise** (in which oxygen is used directly to combine with food fuels to produce energy) at altitude. If the pO_2 levels in arterial blood are markedly reduced, while pH and pCO_2 are held constant, an increase in ventilation occurs.

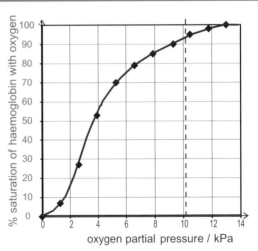

figure 1.24 – the oxyhaemoglobin dissociation curve

Adaptations to respiratory systems at altitude

During the first Global Games to be held at altitude (2240m) at the Mexico Olympic Games in 1968, African athletes who lived at altitude won all the track events at 1500m and over, with the world record holders (who were sea level dwellers) running a lot slower than their best.

- What happens is that residents at altitude are found to have between 12% and 50% more haemoglobin per unit of blood than sea level residents.
- Also, sea level residents who travel to altitude are found to **adapt** by producing more Hb at a rate of between 1% and 2% per week.

- This is done by **increased manufacture of red blood cells** (erythropoietin production).
- Also, there is a **reduction in plasma volume**, a slower long-term adaptation to living at altitude.

- The effect of these **two** factors is to increase the haemoglobin **concentration** in the blood flowing to active tissue, and hence the oxygen-carrying capacity of the blood.

This is why endurance athletes (long distance runners, cyclists or tri-athletes) nowadays try to spend a period of time before competitions living and training at altitude – before returning to sea level, where the extra oxygen carrying capacity of their blood would help improve the intensity and duration of aerobic activity.

Further adaptations occur within tissue cells (see figure 1.25) when low pressure air (and hence oxygen) is breathed:
- There is an increase of up to 16% in **myoglobin** content within muscle cells.
- There is also an increase in numbers of **mitochondria** and **oxidative enzymes** (such as **pyruvate dehydrogenase**) within the **mitochondria** to improve the working capacity of muscles.

- This happens because the efficiency of gaseous exchange improves **within muscle cells** for the sea level dweller that spends some time at altitude.
- Hence he or she would improve **aerobic** athletic performance and oxygen recovery after exercise.

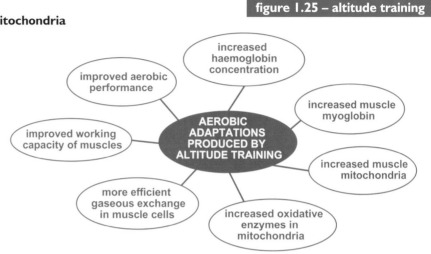

figure 1.25 – altitude training

increased haemoglobin concentration

improved aerobic performance

improved working capacity of muscles

AEROBIC ADAPTATIONS PRODUCED BY ALTITUDE TRAINING

increased muscle myoglobin

increased muscle mitochondria

more efficient gaseous exchange in muscle cells

increased oxidative enzymes in mitochondria

Altitude training

Assuming that you are not training to be a world class runner, what is important for you to realise is that exercising at higher altitudes will **impair** your performance. This is especially true for skiers, campers and hikers.

- **Short-term symptoms** to altitude exposure include headaches and dizziness and increased breathing and heart rates. The key is to adjust gradually (acclimatise) to higher altitude. Hence initial activity should be shorter and less intense when compared with your normal sea level performances.
- The effect of altitude on **anaerobic** athletic activity (sprinting, weightlifting and so on) is minimal since there is no short-term demand for oxygen in these activities.
- There could be a small effect on sprinting and sprint cycling due to the reduced air pressure and hence reduced drag (air resistance) as the athlete's body passes through the air. This effect would improve performance – and was demonstrated by the fact of World records at 100m, 200m, 400m, long jump, and triple jump in the men's track and field events at the Mexico Olympics of 1968.

- Hence altitude training is a predominantly **endurance-based exercise programme** used by elite endurance athletes from a range of sports, consisting of 2 visits (of at least two weeks duration per visit) to altitude (normally between 1800-3000 metres), with the second visit just prior to major competition.
- This will stimulate production of more **haemoglobin** and bigger increases in **myoglobin**, mitochondria and oxidative enzymes than at sea level in the way outlined above and in figure 1.25.

- Hence on return to sea level we have an **increased $\dot{V}O_{2max}$** and tissue cell respiration, leading to enhanced aerobic performance.
- The optimum time to compete is within 3 days of return to sea-level. After this, the adaptations gradually return to sea-level norms over a period of weeks depending on the time spent at altitude, and the individual's basic physiological state.

Hypobaric (hypoxic) chambers or houses

figure 1.26 – a hypoxic tent - sleep high, train low!

This recent development uses dwelling places which use **low-oxygen environments** (hypobaric means low pressure) to simulate altitude training.

An athlete will live and sleep in a hypobaric house situated at sea level, and will train and exercise outside the chamber (at normal oxygen levels, and in his or her normal training environment). This has the effect of elevating EPO, red blood cell levels (hence haemoglobin), myoglobin, mitochondria and oxidative enzymes in a similar way to altitude training.

Hypobaric chambers are used by distance runners, triathletes and endurance cyclists.

A more recent development is the **hypoxic tent**. This is a less expensive system in which a tent is infused with low oxygen air (extra nitrogen infused) but at normal sea-level pressures. Hence a sportsperson can sleep in a tent and gain hypoxic adaptations while asleep (figure 1.26).

Practice questions

1) a) From a physiological standpoint, explain why warm-up is important within an exercise regime.   8 marks

   b) Stretching is a key element in any warm-up. Using an example, identify **two** other elements of a warm-up and explain how they help to prepare an athlete.   4 marks

   c) Describe **three** different methods of stretching and state a sport that would benefit most from each type. 6 marks

2) Define energy, and briefly describe how energy is released from food in the body.   5 marks

3) a) Prescribe a prudent recommendation for approximate percentages of protein, lipid and carbohydrate intake for a general all-round athletic performer.   3 marks

   b) Suggest some general dietary guidelines you would give to a gymnast who is preparing for a major competition.   3 marks

4) Discuss the value of using protein supplementation to enhance performance in power and endurance events.   4 marks

5) What is creatine and how does creatine supplementation improve anaerobic power?   4 marks

6) Briefly describe the process of carbohydrate degradation to re-create energy in the form of adenosine tri-phosphate (ATP).   12 marks

7) Discuss the influence of dietary carbohydrates (CHO) and fats on muscle glycogen stores.   5 marks

8) a) Discuss how a balanced diet could be manipulated to increase an athlete's glucose reserves prior to a marathon race.   6 marks

   b) Carbohydrates are used as an energy source during both aerobic and anaerobic conditions. It is therefore beneficial that an elite athlete's stores of carbohydrate are at a maximum before competition day. Discuss the advantages and disadvantages of glycogen loading.   4 marks

   c) How can an athlete's diet aid the recovery process?   2 marks

9) Describe how an athlete is able to control his or her body temperature during a marathon race.   4 marks

10) What are the major avenues for loss of body heat energy?
    Which of these four pathways is important for controlling body temperature at rest, and during exercise?   6 marks

11) Why is humidity an important factor when an athlete is performing in high temperatures? Why are wind and cloud cover important?   4 marks

12) What is meant by heat acclimatisation? Outline the **main** physiological adaptations which occur to allow an athlete to acclimatise to training and competition at high temperatures.   8 marks

13) Describe the conditions at altitude that could limit performance.   3 marks

14) Describe the major physiological responses and adaptations that accompany acclimatisation to altitude over a period of three weeks.   10 marks

15) What is meant by the concept 'living high and training low'? Identify **two** advantages of using this acclimatisation method.   6 marks

CHAPTER 2: *Short-term psychological preparation*

Motivation and stress control

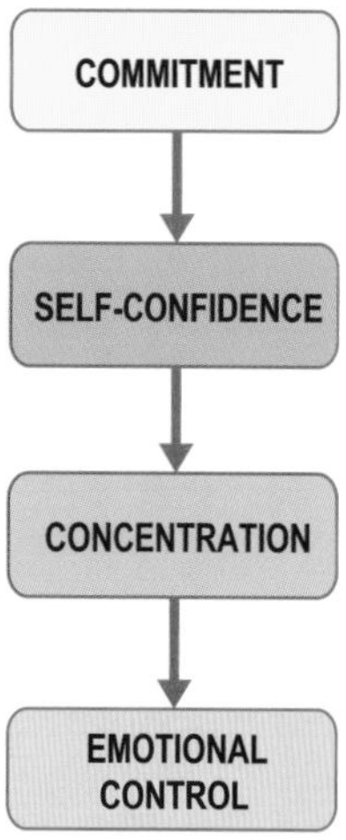

Confidence

Confidence is an element of mental preparation for sports performance, as outlined in figure 2.1. The explanation of how confidence affects us includes:

*   It arouses **positive** emotions.
*   It facilitates **concentration**.
*   It enables **focus** on the important aspects of a task.

figure 2.1 – mental preparation for sports performance

COMMITMENT
↓
SELF-CONFIDENCE
↓
CONCENTRATION
↓
EMOTIONAL CONTROL

figure 2.2 – self-confidence and self-efficacy

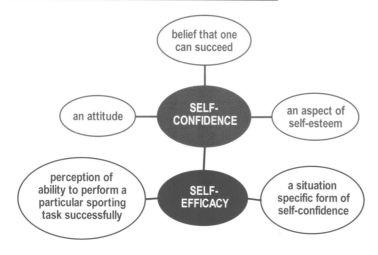

belief that one can succeed — an attitude — SELF-CONFIDENCE — an aspect of self-esteem — perception of ability to perform a particular sporting task successfully — SELF-EFFICACY — a situation specific form of self-confidence

Self-confidence is a feature of a sportsperson's attitude to his or her sporting activity which boosts personal self-worth and self-belief as outlined in figure 2.2. This belief centres around the notion that he or she can win or perform well.

Self-efficacy is a situational form of self-confidence. It is specific to the sport or activity which a person is undertaking.

Confidence (figure 2.3) arouses positive emotions which allow the athlete to:

*   Remain **calm** under pressure.
*   Be **assertive** when required.
*   **Concentrate** easily.
*   **Focus** on the important aspects of a task.
*   Set challenging but realistic **goals**.
*   Increase **effort**.
*   Derive effective game **strategies**.
*   Keep psychological **momentum**.

A confident player plays to win even if it means **taking risks**, will take each point or play at a time, and **never gives up** even when defeat is imminent.

figure 2.3 – self-confidence

calm — assertive — positive — concentration — playing to win — CONFIDENCE — focus — taking risks — realistic goals — never give up — effort

Self-efficacy

Bandura's self-efficacy model (figure 2.4) outlines **four** factors relevant to the self-efficacy of a sports performer.

*   **Performance accomplishments**
    Performance accomplishments consist of **past experiences**, for example, a previously performed skill at dribbling a soccer ball. If this is successful, then this leads to greater self-efficacy at this particular task in the future.

- **Vicarious experiences**
  Vicarious experiences consist of what has **been observed in others** performing a similar skill (the sports performer experiences the same feelings of mastery and competence by watching another person perform a skill as if he or she has performed the skill himself or herself). For example, observing another player in your team dribbling a soccer ball. This is most effective if the model is of similar age or ability and is successful. This process may lead to greater self-efficacy.

figure 2.4 – self-efficacy (Bandura)

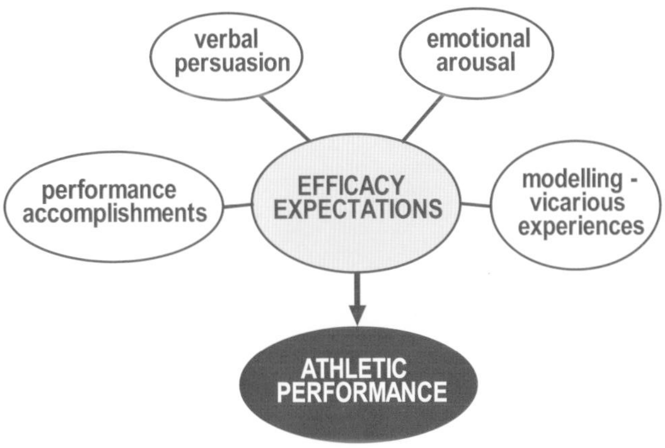

- **Verbal persuasion**
  Verbal encouragement can lead to greater self-efficacy if the person giving encouragement is of **high status** compared with the performer.

- **Emotional arousal**
  If **arousal** is too high, then **state anxiety** (anxiety produced by the specific situation of an activity - otherwise known as **A-state**) can be too high. This could lead to low self-efficacy. Mental rehearsal or physical relaxation techniques could lead to greater confidence and a calmer approach - this also contributes to self-efficacy.

Anxiety

Anxiety can be explained as an emotional state similar to fear, associated with:
- **Physiological** (**somatic**) arousal - connected with raised heart rate, raised breathing rate, sweating and so on.
- **Psychological** (**cognitive**) arousal - worry and negative feelings about the situation, feelings of nervousness.
- Feelings of **apprehension**.

It can have **behavioural** consequences - in which a person will experience:
- **Tension**.
- **Agitation**.
- **Restlessness**.

Trait anxiety - A-trait (Speilberger)
Trait anxiety is an inbuilt (**trait**) **part of the personality** and gives a person:
- A tendency to be **fearful** of unfamiliar situations.
- A tendency to perceive competitive situations as **threatening**.
- A tendency to respond to competitive situations with **apprehension** and **tension**.

State anxiety - A-state
State anxiety is an emotional response to a **particular situation**, characterised by feelings of nervousness and apprehension which is often **temporary** - as you might expect if the anxiety is related to a certain situation which of course will change as daily activities change.

Anxiety and arousal
Arousal is a state of **mental** and **physical preparedness for action**. It is the level of inner drives which forces the sportsperson to **strive to achieve**. It needs to be under control and at the right level depending on the task. Arousal has **somatic** and **cognitive** consequences as outlined above, is similar to the human response to danger, and is **closely linked** to anxiety.

The **reticular activating system** is a system within the brain which causes arousal:
- **Extroverts** have **lower** levels of **intrinsic arousal** than introverts, hence extroverts seek situations of **high arousal**.
- **Introverts** seek low arousal situations.

Theories linking anxiety, arousal and performance

Drive theory

This theory (figure 2.5) describes the simple situation where the **higher** the **arousal** level, the **higher** the achievement or **performance** level.

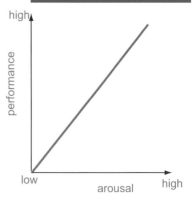

figure 2.5 – drive theory

- Drive theory applies to **gross skills** like weight lifting and sprinting.
- The theory also states that the more arousal, the more likely that a **well-learned** skill (a **dominant response**) will be reproduced.
- This means that older, more deep-seated skills will tend to be produced when a person is very aroused rather than newer, less well-learnt skills practised more recently.

- The implication of this is that a **highly aroused performer** will need to focus very hard and direct his or her attention very strongly towards a **desired response**, particularly if this response includes recently learned elements.
- Otherwise the state of arousal will cause the person to regress to an older, less desirable but dominant response.

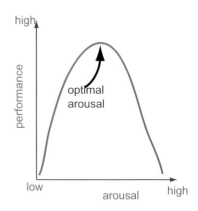

figure 2.6 – inverted U theory

STUDENT NOTE

Drive theory explains why in some sporting activities, a sportsperson who **tries too hard** (and who therefore is in a state of high arousal) fails to reproduce his or her best performance.

Inverted U theory

In **inverted U theory** (figure 2.6) there is an **optimum arousal** level. As arousal increases, performance increases up to a certain point. If aroused more than this, the performance will **go down**.

Optimum arousal depends on:
- **Type of activity**, for example, **gross** skills (like weight lifting) require **high arousal**, whereas **fine** skills (like snooker) require **low arousal**.
- The **skill level of the performer**, the more skilful the performer the **higher** the optimum arousal level could be.
- The **personality of the performer**, in which the more **extrovert** the performer, the **higher** the arousal likely to have to be attained by the performer to produce **optimum** performance.

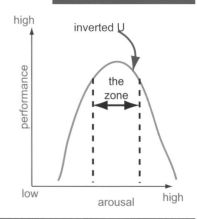

figure 2.7 – the zone

Zone of optimum functioning

An athlete's best performance will be in a **zone** (not just a point of optimum performance - figure 2.7), and different athletes will respond differently to the same arousal situations. They will have **different zones of arousal** for optimum performances depending on **personality**, **skill** or **task** and degree of **habit**. **Habit** is defined as the strength and **permanence** of a correctly learned skill.

Catastrophe theory

Catastrophe theory (see figure 2.8) is a variation of inverted U theory in which performance **increases** as arousal **increases**, but if **arousal** gets **too high** a **complete** loss of performance occurs (the catastrophe).

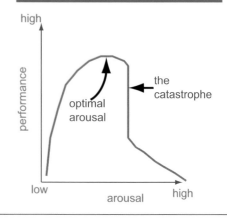

figure 2.8 – catastrophe theory

The performance line on the graph plummets rapidly towards disaster. This almost always happens when the performer **tries too hard**, for example:
- The golfer who tries too hard and completely misses the fairway from his drive at the 18th hole when in a winning position.
- The gymnast who completely messes up her previously well-executed routine.

Anxiety affects arousal, and these theories can also apply to how anxiety affects performance.

Effects of arousal on technique

The **point of optimum arousal** is of crucial importance to the learning and stability of a sportsperson's technique. Technique is the sequence of actions which enables a performer to successfully perform the skill of his or her event. Trying too hard (overarousal) can cause a performer to change his or her technique in an uncontrolled way - with a resultant loss of performance. This can be made worse by the anxiety which would accompany a major event - such as a major at tennis or an open at golf.

Choking and overarousal

High arousal can cause a performer to have negative thoughts. **Negative thoughts of failure** or lack of success can creep in if a performer is **over-aroused**. These thoughts can affect the performer's confidence and create an almost complete inability to perform skills properly. This is **choking** and is an aspect of inverted U theory.

Examples are:
* The snooker player who misses an easy shot when in the final frame of an important match.
* The golfer who misses the fairway from the tee when in the lead in a competition.
* This particularly applies to sports where there is a fine skill.
* Choking can be controlled by **cognitive management techniques** (see page 30 below).

Assertion and aggression

figure 2.9 – aggression or assertion?

* **Assertion** has no intent to harm and uses legitimate force within the rules, displays unusual effort, and may carry unusual energy. This is sometimes called channelled aggression (see figure 2.9).

* **Aggression** (figure 2.10) involves arousal and anger and intention to harm outside the rules.

* **Hostile aggression** has the intent to harm. The goal is to harm with arousal and anger involved.

* **Instrumental aggression** has the intent to harm with the goal to win. This is used as a tactic and is commonly named '**dirty play**'. There is no anger involved and is illegal in all sports except boxing (and other martial arts sports).

figure 2.10 – aggression - the details

- intention to harm another participant, player, spectator or umpire
- verbal aggression if intended to embarrass or hurt
- outside the rules of the sport
- **AGGRESSION**
- not including accidentally injuring or harming
- not including eyeballing or intentionally damaging equipment

Causes of aggression

* **Physiological arousal** in which anger towards another person causes an increase in arousal. This is because the sportsperson is highly motivated.
* **Underdeveloped moral reasoning** in which players with low levels of moral reasoning are more likely to be aggressive.
* **Bracketed morality** in which there is a double standard of condoning aggressive behaviour in sport, but not in life in general. This way of dealing with aggressive behaviour may retard a players' moral development.

Other causes of aggression
- High environmental temperature.
- Home or away.
- Embarrassment.
- Losing.
- Pain.
- Unfair officiating.
- Playing below capability.
- Large score difference.
- Low league standing.
- Later stage of play (near the end of a game).
- Reputation of opposition (get your retaliation in first).

figure 2.11 – theories of aggression

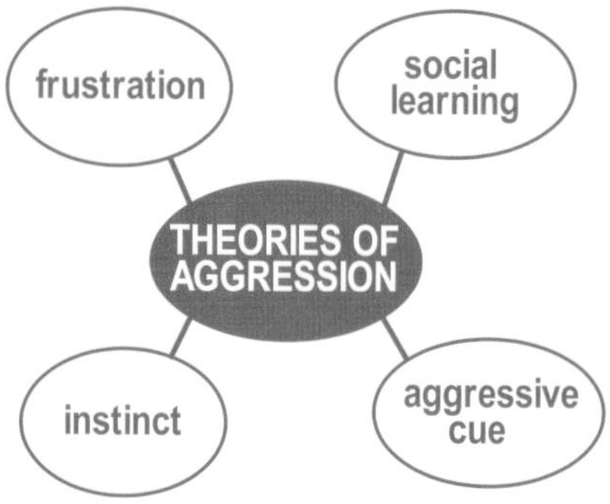

Theories of aggression
- **Instinct theory** (due to Lorentz, figure 2.11) suggests that aggression is innate and instinctive - caused by a 'survival of the species' response to situations as they arise. In this theory, sport releases built-up aggression, and the aggressive response is cathartic - it gets the aggression out of the system, and purges the person of aggressive intent.

- **Frustration aggression theory** (due to Dollard) states that aggression is caused by frustration as the sportsperson is being blocked in the achievement of a goal. This causes a drive towards the source of frustration.

- **Social learning theory** (due to Bandura) suggests that aggression is learned by observation of others' behaviour. Then imitation of this aggressive behaviour is reinforced by social acceptance of the behaviour.

- **Aggressive cue hypothesis** (due to Berkowitz) states that frustration causes anger and arousal which creates a readiness for aggression. The aggression itself can be initiated by an incident during the performance or game (the cue), so that the aggression is a learned response. For example, a player sees a colleague fouled then decides to join in.

Responsibility for aggression
Responsibility for aggression lies within the factors listed in figure 2.12. Influential others can exert a moderating influence on the performer, but the performer must accept that aggression is the wrong thing to do, and modify behaviour accordingly. **Reinforcement** of good behaviour will be important to ensure behavioural change.

figure 2.12 – responsibility for aggression

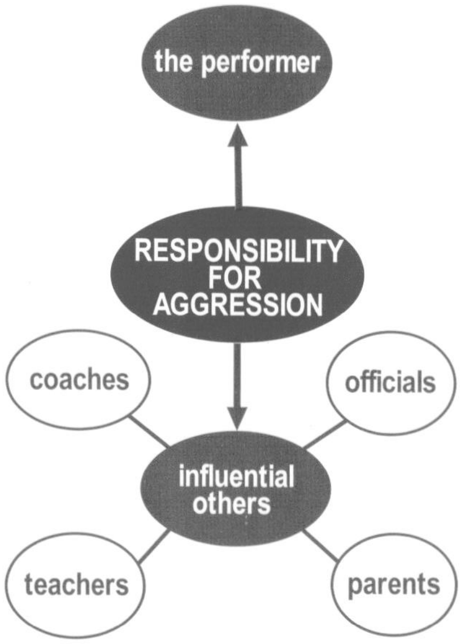

Strategies

The following section looks at the strategies used by sportspeople to improve performance by enabling them to focus or concentrate on the important or relevant elements of performance.

Cognitive techniques - mental rehearsal

Cognitive relaxation and stress management techniques
- **Imagery relaxation** is a technique in which a person will think of a place with associations of warmth and relaxation, and then imagine the activity or skill. This can be practised in non-stressful situations - and used prior to competition.

- **Thought stopping** is a method employed when **negative thoughts** or worry (about failure) begin. The performer should immediately think 'STOP', and substitute a positive thought.

- **Self-talk** involves talking through the process of a competitive situation, talking positively and building self-confidence.

- **Cognitive stress management** involves the control of emotions and thought processes linked to attributions (the reasons for good or poor performances - see page 66 below). This should eliminate negative feelings and develop self-confidence.

Mental practice or rehearsal

Mental rehearsal (figure 2.13) is the mental or cognitive rehearsal of a skill without actual physical movement. It is used by most top level sportsmen to visualise a skill or movement often prompted by tape, film or talk from a coach.

Mental practice or **rehearsal**:

- Creates a **mental picture** of a skill.
- Can be used to **simulate** a whole movement sequence or just part of it.
- Can be used to **imagine** and envisage success and avoid failure in a competitive situation.
- Can provide a mental warm-up in order to promote a state of **readiness** for action.
- Must be as **realistic** as possible to be effective.
- Can be used during **rest** or **recovery** periods **during** a performance or in between performances.
- Can be used to **focus** attention on important aspects of a skill.
- Builds **self-confidence** for an upcoming performance.
- **Controls arousal** and induces calmness before a performance.
- Can be used to enable the learner to **memorise** a skill or movement more effectively.

figure 2.13 – mental rehearsal/practice

USES OF MENTAL PRACTICE

- mental picture of a skill
- imagine success or avoid failure
- mental warm-up, readiness for action
- must be as realistic as possible
- used during rest periods
- prevents wear and tear
- small muscle contractions same as actual practice
- focus attention on important aspects of skill
- building self-confidence
- control arousal before performance
- simulate a whole movement sequence

It works by producing **small muscle contractions** in the same sequence as an actual practice, and since the gross movement of the skill does not actually happen, it **prevents** wear and tear.

Goal setting

Goal setting (see page 64 below for more details) can be a cognitive element of success in sport which is more likely because:
- Learning is **focused**.
- **Uncertainty** is reduced.
- **Confidence** is increased.
- **Practice** is planned and structured.
- Evaluation and **feedback** are specific.

Use of cognitive techniques to assist concentration

Concentration is a state of mind in which attention is directed towards a specific aim or activity. This can be considered as attentional focus in which a performer will have control of attention towards a task. The cognitive techniques used to assist concentration include imagery, mental rehearsal and relaxation. These techniques can be thought to manage the stress of a situation, and to manage anxiety in a productive way.

Attentional control training (ACT) is a personalised programme which targets a performer's specific concentration problems and assesses the demands of the sport, the situation, and the personality of the performer.

Somatic relaxation techniques

Somatic techniques are listed in figure 2.14, and involve use of and control of the physiology of a body.

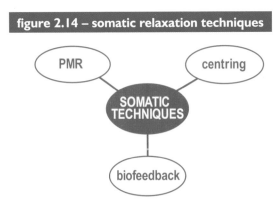

figure 2.14 – somatic relaxation techniques

SOMATIC TECHNIQUES
- PMR
- centring
- biofeedback

Self-directed muscle relaxation training - progressive muscle relaxation - PMR

Within this technique, a performer focuses on each of the major muscle groups in turn, and allows breathing to become slow and easy. He or she will **visualise** the **tension flowing out** of a muscle group until he or she is completely relaxed. Eventually he or she will be able to combine muscle groups and achieve **total relaxation** quickly.

Centring

Centring involves **control of physiological symptoms** of stress by focusing on control of the diaphragm and deep breathing.

Biofeedback

This is a set of techniques which monitor and interpret various physiological indicators:

- **Skin temperature** which tells us that the skin is cold if stressed, and warm if unstressed.
- **Galvanic skin response**, in which electrical conductivity of the skin is measured, which increases when moist (tense muscle causes sweating).
- **Electromyography**, in which electrodes are taped to specific muscles which can detect electrical activity within the muscle and hence its tension.

Control of aggressive behaviour

Governing bodies

Governing bodies are responsible for **player codes of conduct** which should involve coaches, players and officials. They will:
- Use strong officials where appropriate.
- Alter rules of games and implement punishment (remove league points, use sin bins) and so on.
- Reward non-aggressive acts (for example, the FIFA fair play award).
- Will encourage suitable use of language.
- Attempt to reduce media sensationalism in connection with aggression on or off the field of play.

A coach education programme is essential to reduce and control aggressive behaviour among players.

Coaches and players

- Coaches and players (figure 2.15) should promote ethical and sporting behaviour.
- They should control aggressive behaviour using stress management strategies and **relaxation techniques** among players.
- Coaches should initiate **self-control** strategies, and attempt to reduce levels of arousal in players.

- Both coaches and players should maintain a **healthy will-to-win** without winning being everything, and set **performance goals** rather than outcome goals.

- Coaches should **remove players** from the field if it is determined that he or she (but usually he!) is at risk of aggression.
- Their tactic would be to enable **channelling of aggression** towards a performance goal, and use **peer pressure** to 'avoid letting the side down'.

figure 2.15 – controlling aggression?

External influences

Social facilitation

Social facilitation concerns how people other than the performer can influence his or her attitudes and behaviour.

The effect that the presence of spectators has on the way sportspeople play or perform can be positive (called **facilitation**), or negative (called **inhibition**). For example, a crowd (figure 2.16) encourages a team playing well (positive or facilitation), or the crowd jeers at a team not playing well (negative or inhibition).

Facilitation

Facilitation of a performance by an audience tends to lead to the fact that high arousal leads to improved performance by a highly skilled or extrovert performer. Gross or simple skills tend to be improved by audience effects. See the link between arousal and performance in drive theory (see page 28 above).

figure 2.16 – effects of audience?

Inhibition

Where the presence of an audience **inhibits performance**, high arousal tends to lead to reduced performance by novices whose skills are not well-learned. This also applies to introvert performers. Fine and complex skills requiring great concentration will also tend to have performance levels reduced by negative audience effects.

Different types of audience

Passive others (social facilitation) are audience and co-actors, and **interactive others** are competitors and spectators.

Co-actors

Co-actors are a passive form of audience involved in the same activity and at the same time as the performer, but not competing directly. For example:

* Officials, umpires or referees.
* Members of a player's own team.
* Ball-boys (figure 2.17) or helpers during a performance.

figure 2.17 – ball-boys as co-actors

Factors affecting performance

* **Size of audience** - larger crowds create more arousal.
* **Proximity of audience** - the closer the audience the greater the arousal.
* **Intentions of the audience** - can be positive or negative. If spectators are negative about a player (shouting or jeering) this may suppress arousal or increase arousal depending on the personality of the performer.
* **Skill level** or **difficulty** of the task - performance improves for a well-learned skill and decreases if the skill is not well-learned.
* **Personality** of the performer - extroverts perform better when aroused, but introverts can be over-aroused.
* **Type of task** (figure 2.18) - fine skills need lower levels of arousal whereas gross skills could be improved by increased arousal.

figure 2.18 – fine skills or gross skills

Zajonc's model

Zajonc's theory says that the mere **presence of others** creates **arousal**, which then affects performance negatively if a skill is poorly-learnt (early in the learning curve - figure 2.19).

In this case, arousal causes an incorrect response because the incorrect response is dominant.

On the other hand, if a skill is **well-learnt** (later in the learning curve), then **arousal** causes a **correct response** because the correct response is dominant.

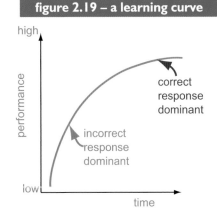

figure 2.19 – a learning curve

high

performance

correct
response
dominant

incorrect
response
dominant

low

time

Evaluation apprehension

This theory (due to Cottrell - figure 2.20) explains that an **audience is perceived as evaluating** (assessing the value or worth) of performance. This **causes anxiety** - which in turn causes arousal.

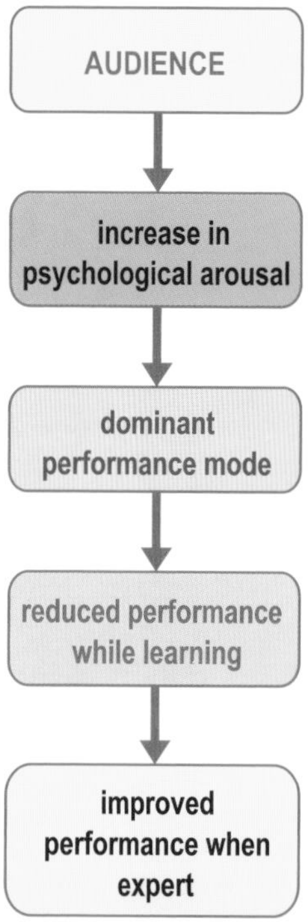

Coping strategies include:
- Stress management.
- Mental rehearsal.
- Selective attention (away from evaluators).
- Lowering the importance of the situation.
- Training with an audience present.

STUDENT NOTE

Look at inverted-U theory for the connection between arousal and performance (see page 28 above).

figure 2.20 – the process of evaluation apprehension

The distraction effect

Distraction is an aspect of concentration (or **lack of concentration**). Attentional focus is very important for the effective sportsperson and if this is disrupted then he or she is distracted from his or her task. Audience and evaluation apprehension can act as a distraction. The sportsperson needs therefore to practise in distracting circumstances, and practise switching attentional focus when faced with potentially distracting circumstances.

Homefield advantage

Home or away effect on performance concerns the fact that more teams win at home than away.

A crowd may be judged as supportive or hostile (facilitation or inhibition), and high levels of anxiety caused by hostility may reduce performance.

The environment of their own stadium or playing situation is familiar to home teams, therefore home players are more comfortable. This limits anxiety and enables a worry free and hopefully successful performance (figure 2.21).

figure 2.21 – World Cup 1966 - Wembley, 97,000 spectators, homefield advantage?

Practice questions

1) a) What is meant by the term self-efficacy when applied to sports psychology?
   1 mark

   b) Bandura suggested that self-efficacy is influenced by **four** factors. Identify and apply these factors to a sport of your choice.
   8 marks

   c) As a coach of a sports team, how would you raise an individual's level of self-efficacy?
   4 marks

2) A number of PE students are attending trials at their chosen sport. Describe the Inverted U theory and explain how it might affect a student's performance at the trials.
   5 marks

3) a) Discuss the possible relationships between anxiety and performance in sporting activities.
   12 marks

   b) High levels of arousal have often been linked with stress. Sketch a graph showing the relationship between the performance of a complex skill and level of arousal.
   2 marks

   c) Add a second curve to your graph showing how the performance of a simple skill might be affected by arousal.
   2 marks

4) With reference to sporting performance, explain how cognitive and somatic anxiety differ.   5 marks

5) Outline and suggest strategies to aid mental short-term preparation.   8 marks

6) a) What do we mean by the term aggression in sports psychology? Give an example from a sport or game which would illustrate your answer.   2 marks

    b) Using examples from sport, briefly describe the differences between aggression and assertion?   2 marks

    c) Some team players display unwanted aggression. What are the possible causes of such aggression?   4 marks

7) a) Explain in more detail what is meant by social learning when applied to aggression.   4 marks

    b) How can aggressive tendencies be eliminated in a sports situation?   4 marks

8) a) The aggressive cue hypothesis (Berkowitz 1969), is a theory which explains why aggression may be experienced by sports performers. Using an example from sport, describe the aggressive cue hypothesis.   4 marks

    b) Using examples from sport, explain the frustration-aggression hypothesis.   4 marks

9) Discuss how theories of aggression can be applied to sport.   6 marks

10) a) What is meant by social facilitation and what is its main effect?   3 marks

     b) What effects can be experienced by an individual if there is an audience present?   6 marks

11) a) What is meant by evaluation apprehension?   2 marks

     b) As a coach of an individual who is affected adversely by the presence of an audience, how would you help him or her to overcome the negative influences?   4 marks

12) Two groups of male sportspeople (of the same age) undertook an arms length weight hold endurance test. Success at this exercise was measured by the length of time the weight was held. Table 2.1 below shows the average times for group 1 (who did the exercise alone) and group 2 (who did the exercise in the presence of an audience).

Table 2.1 – **time for a weight hold endurance test**

	group 1 no audience	group 2 with audience
average time held in seconds	46.5	50.5

     a) What effect (if any) did the audience have on the performance of the exercise?   1 mark

     b) How would you account for this effect (or lack of effect)?   4 marks

     c) The audience in this exercise (for group 2) was not known to the participants. Explain any effect you think there would be if the audience was known to the group.   6 marks

13) Using examples from sport, explain what is meant by evaluation apprehension and outline the causes of it.   3 marks

CHAPTER 3: *Short-term technical preparation*

Kit and equipment

Kit and equipment selection

Kit will be selected according to the environmental factors listed in figure 3.1.

Environmental factors

Climate
Athletes need to select the appropriate kit that helps them to maintain a constant core temperature.

Figure 3.2 outlines the sorts of clothing appropriate to rain and wind, cold weather, and hot conditions.

Wind increases heat loss by convection and is known as the wind chill factor.

High humidity limits sweat evaporation and heat loss.

Clothing fabrics such as Gore-Tex do not let rain in from the outside, but allow moisture (sweat) to pass through from the inner side, and so are favoured outfits in wet and cold conditions.
Wicking fabrics, which are a mixture of cotton and man-made fibres, have the ability to soak up sweat then move it away from the body, saving energy on maintaining skin temperature.
In hot conditions, one of the reasons why female athletes wear near-bikini type outfits (figure 3.2) is to aid evaporation of sweat from the large surface area of exposed skin.

Specialist clothing
- Lycra sports clothing **reduces air resistance**.
- Special **shark suits** for the swimmers - **reduce drag**.
- Swim hats reduce drag on the head (fluid dynamics - figure 3.3).
- Compression clothing (rubber belts or strapping) to **increase hydrostatic pressure** within a body part (figure 3.4) - one shoulder javelin suit, and bench press and squatting suits.
- The force from the belt supports the tissue enclosed from the inside.

The shark suit dilemma
At the 2009 World swimming championships, almost every race produced a World record swim (from 50m fly to 1500m freestyle).

The suits being used were essentially wetsuits with four characteristics:
- High **compression**, hence **better venous return** and **recovery**. The suits took up to 40 minutes to get into, causing problems with check-in and warm-up.
- **Teflon coated**, so that the **drag was reduced** by between 2 and 5%.
- **Air trapping** which gave the suit extra **buoyancy** and caused the swimmer to have less surface in contact with the water (more body showing above the water surface), and hence **less drag**.
- The **cost**, at up to £1000 for three or four swims. This means that there was a financial penalty placed on non-elite swimmers without National support.
The suits have been banned from the end of the 2009 season - will World performances fall?

figure 3.1 – environmental factors

climate temperature, humidity, wind	playing surface ash, grass, astroturf, mondo

ENVIRONMENTAL FACTORS

protection injury prevention	indoor or outdoor roofed stadium or open

figure 3.2 – clothing for conditions

figure 3.3 – streamlined swim hats

figure 3.4 – compression strapping

Specialist training clothing or strapping

There are a few such items which can be used in training, but are **not allowed** in competition situations, for example:

* Strapping a shot putter's fingers or hand (the event is supposed to be performed without artificial aids to the hand).
* Hooks or metal within a hammer thrower's glove.
* Artificial springs within running shoes (except for disabled athletes in certain categories).
* Hand straps in weights lifting (wrist straps are allowed in competition).
* Weights attached to the feet in the athletic throwing events.
* Weights held in the hand in jumping events.

Protective clothing

Protective clothing ranges from wetsuits to winter sports, hikers' outfits and specialist protective clothing needed in many of the sports listed below. Protective clothing reduces the risk of injury from impact, playing surfaces and environmental conditions depending on the nature of the sport.

* Fencing (figure 3.5).
* Ice hockey.
* Field hockey.
* Cricket.
* Baseball.
* Rugby.
* American football.
* Equestrianism.
* Boxing.

figure 3.5 – specialist protection clothing

Clothing - footwear

Boots provide foot stability in many sports, since ankle breaks and sprains are very common sports injuries, particularly in:

* Basketball.
* Skiing or snow boarding (figure 3.6).
* Many sports where cushioning from running shoes or trainers can provide protection against foot impact injuries such as stress fractures and shin soreness.
* Most athletes will have had orthotic assessment for shoe inserts which will correct foot posture. Shoe orthotics are now made by computer.

figure 3.6 – ski-boots protect ankles

Sports shoes incorporate the latest wicking and breathing technology to give comfort, lightness and strength.

Playing surface - indoor or outdoor?

Over the last 30 years synthetic playing surfaces have spread throughout the world. These surfaces have reduced the element of chance, speeding games up and rewarding skill. For example, tennis players preparing for a hard court tournament, such as the US Open, know that the hard playing surface will hardly change from one venue to the next and hence their matches will be more predictable. Some sports have retained their natural playing surfaces. For example, cricket can have cracked, fast or slow surfaces, and grass tennis courts can be threadbare or lush. Playing surface variables such as this affect speed of play, elements of surprise, and reward skill.

Athletes need to assess their playing surfaces and environments, and adjust their game (and kit) accordingly.

For example, the shiny new retractable roof for Wimbledon centre court (see figure 3.7) can cut out unpleasantly cold, blustery and wet conditions to provide still air and ambient adjustable temperatures.

In the short-term, players need to adjust to their conditions. They will get used to the amplified sound of play such as public address systems and ball on racket impact, and light conditions.

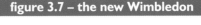

figure 3.7 – the new Wimbledon

Design of kit or equipment

Figure 3.8 outlines the cultural and utility criteria upon which kit or equipment are designed world-wide.

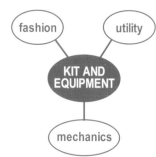

figure 3.8 – design of kit and equipment

Fashion

Provided that basic decency is maintained within the rules of a sport, fashion can dictate the shape, colour, and dimensions of kit worn.
For example:
* The Nike Rafa clothing (figure 3.9) and shoes worn by Rafael Nadal.
* Swimwear as worn by our World and Olympic champions.
* Jogging and track wear as worn by top athletes.
* Golf kit as worn by Tiger Woods.

Utility

The design of kit and equipment must meet the requirements of the sport for which it is intended. However, experiments are regularly made by manufacturers to sports shoes, for example:
* Multiple spikes to track shoes.
* Thickness of sole for rock climbing boots and throwing shoes.
* Studs on soccer and rugby boots (length and number).

Examples of other items of clothing:
* Strength of the material in rugby shorts and shirts.
* Stretchability of material used in tennis or athletics wear.

figure 3.9 – RAFA fashion?

Mechanics

The design of kit and equipment must meet the requirements of the **mechanics** of the sport for which it is intended. Equipment is designed to enable forces to be applied to the body or playing materials in the most efficient manner.

For example:
* **Swimwear** shape and surface characteristics - reduce fluid friction drag (see page 36).
* Swim and cycling **headwear** - reduce fluid friction drag (fluid dynamics).
* The **streamlined** clothing, hat and position by Graeme Obree to reduce fluid friction (fluid dynamics) - Graeme Obree redesigned the **standard racing bike** and broke many World records because the bike was more efficient (figure 3.10).
* **Rigidity and studding** or spiking of sports footwear.
* **Cushioning** of the sole of sports footwear to prevent injury and increase foot-time contact.
* **Sticky surfaces** to rugby balls to increase friction between ball and hand.

figure 3.10 – Graeme Obree's bike - a mechanical design

Compression clothing

Research has shown that compression clothing (figure 3.11) will **increase venous return** and $\dot{V}O_{2max}$ during **high intensity exercise**.

Loughborough University and Canterbury (sport clothing) showed that a 2.7% increase in **peak power** could be achieved in short periods of high intensity cycle ergometer testing. This has the effect of improving the performance of rugby and other team players, and when worn after training, recovery is improved and DOMS reduced.

figure 3.11 – compression clothing

Ergogenic aids for short-term preparation

An **ergogenic aid** is any substance or method which enhances performance. This includes any method used in training which has this effect including training equipment and nutrition as well as doping and supplementation. Some drugs fall into this definition, and they are briefly listed in table 3.1. You will find more detail on page 118 of AS Revise PE for Edexcel, ISBN: 978 1 901424 54 6.

Drugs and supplements

Table 3.1 – **the categories of substances used in top level sport today**

types of substance	effects
stimulants	increase alertness, reduce fatigue, increase competitiveness and hostility
narcotics & analgesics	management of severe pain
anabolic steroids	increase muscle strength and bulk, promote aggressiveness
diuretics	reduce weight quickly, reduce concentration of substances by diluting urine, masking agent
peptide & glycoprotein hormones & analogues	growth hormone and regulation of red blood cell production (example: rEPO, HGH)
creatine & supplements	not drugs but health risks with excessive use

See pages 117-119 of AS Revise PE for Edexcel, ISBN: 978 1 901424 54 6.

Blood doping
Blood doping is an illegal method which comes under the heading of 'doping' but which does not involve ingestion of illegal substances.

Blood doping involves the removal of an athlete's own blood which is then stored. The athlete's body then remanufactures blood to replace that taken, then the stored blood is reinfused. This temporarily increases red blood cell count (polycythemia), but has the potential problem of mis-matching which can lead to a transfusion reaction. This process **increases VO$_{2max}$** and hence energy delivery to enhance aerobic performances.

Ergogenic aids
Dietary manipulation such as carboloading within a nutritional programme has been discussed above on page 18.

Figure 3.12 outlines the different types of legal ergogenic aid, some of which are discussed below.

Psychological
Even products like **creatine** (see page 20 above) can put the body in a highly motivated state. Much has been made of the **physiological** effects, but the impact of **psychological** factors can sometimes be overlooked.

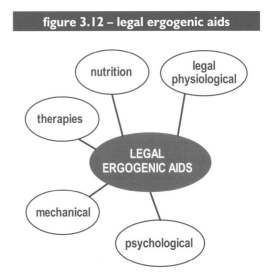

figure 3.12 – legal ergogenic aids

Examples of legal physiological supplements, aids or methods

- **Creatine** supplementation is a method of boosting the ATP-PC system of ATP regeneration during anaerobic exercise, and has been discussed on page 20 above.

- **Glutamine** is an **amino acid** forming part of **skeletal muscle** and **immune cells**. Supplementation after exercise therefore reinforces the immune system and **reduces the risk of infection** and therefore enhances the process of glycogen synthesis in recovering muscles.

- For endurance-based athletes, **altitude training** often precedes climatic acclimatisation, see page 24 above.

- **Fluid intake** has almost become an obsession with modern sportsmen and women. Modern athletes frequently use isotonic sports drinks, such as Isostar and Red Bull, just prior to competition to maintain rehydration and alertness respectively.

- **Bicarbonate loading** is a process whereby a performer ingests bicarbonate prior to a competition. An athlete can increase plasma bicarbonate levels that provide additional buffering capacity, thus allowing higher concentrations of lactate in the blood. Theoretically, this could delay the onset of fatigue in all-out anaerobic activity such as a 400 metre race. Bicarbonate loading can cause cramping, vomiting, bloating and diarrhoea.

Therapies as legal ergogenic aids

- **Physiotherapy** and **herbal medicines** can be used in injury treatment, and also used to reduce muscle soreness (DOMS) and aid recovery of local damaged tissue.

- **Sports massage** is the skilled manipulation of soft tissue for the relief and treatment of muscle soreness and pain and the maintenance of muscle balance and improved flexibility. Athletes can benefit from sports massage before, during and after the event.

- **Acupuncture** is a technique of inserting and manipulating fine filiform needles into specific points on the body to relieve pain or for therapeutic purposes.

- **Ice baths** and **ice belts** are used to reduce joint and muscle inflammation produced by microtears in tissue affected by intense training.

- Ice or **cooling jackets** are used to attempt to reduce core temperature of sports participants in very hot conditions.

For example:
- Tennis players in long hot matches.
- Paula Radcliffe just before starting a marathon.
- Australian rowing 8 in Atlanta Olympic Games 1996 (figure 3.13).

figure 3.13 – use of ice jackets in a competitive situation

Mechanical ergogenic aids

- **Nasal strips** use sticky plaster placed over the bridge of the nose to enlarge the nasal cavity which enables easier breathing (figure 3.14).
- **Carbon fibre bike frames** are lighter and aerodynamically more efficient, and bike helmets are shaped to reduce drag (air resistance).
- **Specialist training machines** specific to the sport.
- **Resistance training equipment** such as weight training machines or pulley machines.
- **Hypobaric** (low pressure, low oxygen or hypoxic) chambers, to have similar effects as altitude training (see page 24 above).
- **Specialist clothing** to reduce drag.
- **Compression clothing**, and specialist training items.

figure 3.14 – Paula Radcliffe uses nasal strips

STUDENT NOTE

The details of these ergogenic aids are discussed on page 82 onwards below.

Use of holding camps - pre-match rituals

Holding Camps

It has been the habit within most major sports in the UK to have holding camps **prior to major games** (World Championships or Olympic Games). The reason for this is to allow **acclimatisation** to local conditions before the games actually start - this is a short-term issue which adds hugely to the well-being of sportspeople. Recent examples include:

- The holding camp in Macau (near Hong Kong) for teamGB just before the Beijing Olympics 2008.
- The holding camp in Cyprus just before the Athens Olympics 2004.

Athletes are transported from the holding camp to the games just before they are due to perform.

- This avoids the hassle of fighting for **training facilities** with every other athlete in the world.
- The athletes can be serviced by their **coaches** and **medical teams** right up to the crucial point, noting that there is often not room for this detailed support in the games environment itself.
- It is aimed at having **conditions of temperature and humidity** as similar as possible to the games environment, as well as the time zone - which is to avoid jet-lag.
- Training facilities are usually excellent, allowing athletes to settle into a **'comfort-zone'** of lifestyle and **routine**, which can lead to peace of mind prior to the excitement of the games itself.

figure 3.15 – Macau for teamGB - note the rain

Unfortunately, the Macau camp was interrupted by a tropical typhoon and lots of rain (figure 3.15), so temperatures were lower than expected, and training conditions less than ideal. But the team gained in 'team spirit', were able to sort out dietary issues (some athletes are notoriously fussy eaters), and improve the 'feel-good factor'.

Unfortunately, several athletes got food poisoning - in spite of teamGB having its own chef and dedicated kitchen - this is always a risk when athletes travel abroad.

Different sports choose different patterns for these camps. For example, the GB cycling team spent this same period (prior to Beijing) in Newport (South Wales - figure 3.16) near a top quality velodrome.

figure 3.16 – the teamGB cycling camp in South Wales

This difference may have been due to the lack of availability of a suitable velodrome in Macau, and the fact that the sport is indoors - hence climate acclimatisation is less important. The team were able to train hard and 'team spirit' and the 'feel-good factor' were high - leaving the acclimatisation until later and no food poisoning!

The teamGB cycling team performed excellently in Beijing.

Pre-match rituals

Individuals have **pre-match rituals** which include warm-up and whose aim is to make the sportsperson ready for the effort of match or competition.

Readiness is psychological and physiological and includes:
- **Calming** or centring routines.
- Improving **awareness of surroundings** and **opponents**.
- Improving **self-confidence** by practising rhythms and skill-related routines.
- **Self-hypnosis** and mental imagery routines.
- Optimising **blood flow to muscles**.

Rituals

Rituals include:

- Chanting and talking (**New Zealand Haka** - figure 3.17).

- Having a highly structured warm-up routine.

- Getting dressed, travelling and preparing equipment in exactly the same way each time.

- Having the same food prepared in the same way each time, which might assist people to avoid food poisoning.

- Rafael Nadal has his drinks bottles carefully positioned - in exactly the same position and order in each match (figure 3.18). It seems important for extreme endurance athletes to have several different drinks with different properties - minerals, energy or water.

figure 3.17 – New Zealand Haka

figure 3.18 – Rafael's rituals

Practice questions

1) Playing kit and equipment are major factors that athletes need to consider in their short-term preparation for sport. Identify the key factors that affect the selection of their use, illustrating your answers with examples.   10 marks

2) What is an ergogenic aid? Briefly provide a summary of the role that nutritional supplements play in improving performance.   8 marks

3) a) Describe the method of blood doping and its potential for improving endurance performance.   4 marks

   b) Why is blood doping an illegal ergogenic aid?   3 marks

4) Give a brief outline and comment upon the following techniques which may be employed in the belief that they will enhance sport performance.

   a) The use of anabolic steroids.   4 marks

   b) The use of creatine supplements.   4 marks

   c) Highlight **two** potential health risks known to be associated with the use of each of these techniques.   4 marks

5) Explain and discuss the use of legal ergogenic aids for short-term preparation in sport.   20 marks

6) Explain how the scientific and social principles behind the use of holding camps can assist in the preparation of elite performers.   20 marks

CHAPTER 4: *Fatigue and the recovery process*

Fatigue

figure 4.1 – an exhausted athlete?

Effects of fatigue on performance

Performance can be affected by muscle fatigue, the depletion of energy stores in muscle (and the liver). Various factors contribute to this.

Muscle fatigue
Muscle fatigue can be described as a reduction of muscular performance, and an inability to maintain expected power output. Performance can often be continued at quite a high level in spite of fatigue, but the outcome of 'jelly legs' or 'jelly shoulders' will be well known to all sportspeople after an exhausting performance has been completed (figure 4.1).

Depletion of energy stores

- Depletion of **PC** (phosphocreatine) and muscle and liver **glycogen** stores will be the major cause of fatigue.
- Fatigue in marathon runners is due to depletion of **muscle glycogen** in both ST and FT muscle fibres.
- **FT muscle fibres** have low aerobic capacity and therefore **quickly fatigue** during maximal activity. This is because stored ATP and PC are quickly used up (in under 7 seconds) during this sort of activity (weight training, sprinting for example).

Metabolic accumulation

During intense exercise lasting longer than 7 seconds and under 45 seconds, **accumulation of lactic acid** and CO_2 in muscle cells causes extreme fatigue and complete loss of muscle function. This is because increase in H^+ ions (decrease in pH due to the lactic acid acidity) inhibits both aerobic and anaerobic enzyme activity required for ATP regeneration.

Central governor theory (St Clair Gibson)

This theory outlines a possible psychological element to fatigue.

- The theory says that **fatigue is a perception**, and is an **emotional response** to situations (particularly of continuous stress or anxiety).
- The theory asserts that the brain interprets muscle fatigue as it progresses during an activity, and **will not allow** the muscle to proceed to complete exhaustion.
- The situation is '**paced**' by the brain, and the sensations of complete fatigue (muscle pain and discomfort) are created by the brain when it really is time to quit.
- The fittest and best prepared athlete will **push this point** until either he or she wins and finishes the activity - or collapses completely.

Body fluid balance and dehydration

- Fluid loss **decreases plasma volume** which reduces blood pressure and hence reduction in blood flow to skin and muscles.
- This means that the heart has to work harder, body temperature rises, and **fatigue** occurs.
- Hence **fluid intake is important** during endurance activities.

Recovery

Bodily processes do not immediately return to resting levels after exercise ceases. The time taken for this to occur is called the **recovery period**. The recovery period is dependent on the intensity and duration of the exercise.

Excess post-exercise oxygen consumption (EPOC)

Factors contributing to EPOC

After every strenuous exercise (figure 4.2), there are **four** tasks that need to be completed before the exhausted muscle can operate at full efficiency again:

- **Replacement of ATP and phosphocreatine** (fast replenishment component).
- **Removal of lactic acid** (slow replenishment component).
- **Replenishment of myoglobin** with oxygen.
- **Replacement of glycogen**.

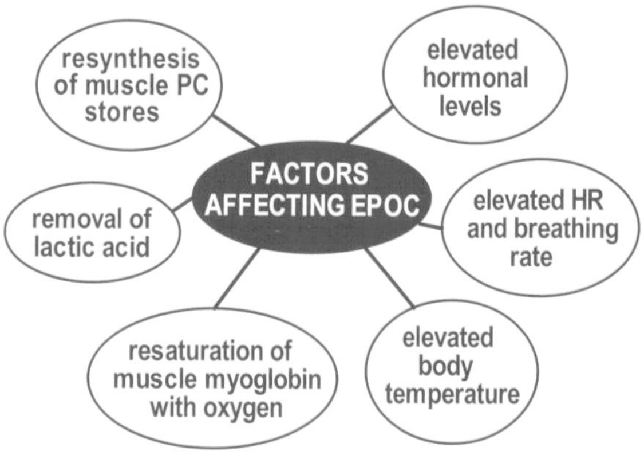

The first three require oxygen in substantial quantities, hence the need for rapid breathing and high pulse rate to carry oxygen to the muscle cells.

The need for oxygen

The need for oxygen to rapidly replace ATP and remove lactic acid is known as the oxygen debt. The more modern term for oxygen debt is **excess post-exercise oxygen consumption** (EPOC) or oxygen recovery. This represents the elevation of the metabolic rate above resting values which occurs after exercise during the recovery period.

EPOC is the excess O_2 consumed following exercise needed to provide the energy required to resynthesise ATP used and remove lactic acid created during previous exercise. EPOC has **two** components (figure 4.3):

- **Alactic or alactacid**.
- **Lactic or lactacid**.

The **oxygen deficit** is the difference between the oxygen required during exercise and the oxygen actually consumed during the activity. The graph in figure 4.3 shows the relationship between oxygen consumption and the time before, during and after exercise.

The alactacid component

This component involves the **conversion of ADP back into PC and ATP**, and is known as **restoration of muscle phosphagen**. This is a very rapid process (120 seconds to full restoration - see figure 4.4) and is of size 2 to 3.5 litres of O_2.

Phosphagen recovery is achieved via **three** mechanisms:

- There is **aerobic** conversion of carbohydrates into CO_2 and H_2O to resynthesise ATP from ADP and P_i.
- Some of the ATP is immediately utilised **to create PC** using the coupled reaction: **ATP + C → ADP + PC**.
- A small amount of ATP is **resynthesised via glycogen,** producing small amounts of lactic acid.

figure 4.2 – factors contributing to EPOC

resynthesis of muscle PC stores · elevated hormonal levels · removal of lactic acid · **FACTORS AFFECTING EPOC** · elevated HR and breathing rate · resaturation of muscle myoglobin with oxygen · elevated body temperature

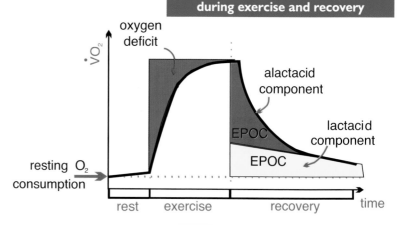

figure 4.3 – oxygen consumption during exercise and recovery

oxygen deficit

$\dot{V}O_2$

alactacid component

EPOC

lactacid component

EPOC

resting O_2 consumption

rest   exercise   recovery   time

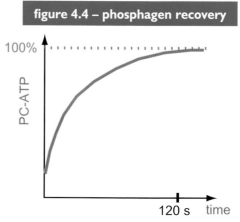

figure 4.4 – phosphagen recovery

100%

PC-ATP

120 s   time

Continuous oxygen recovery

During the **post-exercise period**, oxygen recovery is continuous.

This is because:
- Muscle myoglobin recovers.
- Temperature falls.
- Hormone levels fall.

During the **recovery period**, temperature and hormone levels are higher than normal (although falling), which:
- Keeps metabolic rate high.
- Keeps respiratory rate high.
- Keeps heart rate high.
- Requires more oxygen than normal.

Hence EPOC increases.

The implications for interval training

- If there is only a short interval between bouts of exercise, the level of phosphagen stores gradually reduces (see figure 4.5) thereby reducing the energy available for the later bouts.
- This stresses the ATP and PC storage and forces the muscle cells to adapt by storing more of these quantities.
- Also, cells will adapt by improving their ability to provide O_2, and hence increase the possible size of the alactic component.

- Anaerobic interval training studies have shown that 30s bouts of exercise increase the activities of **glycolytic enzymes**, such as phosphorylase, phosphofructokinase and lactate dehydrogenase from around 10% to 25%.
- This increase in **glycolytic capacity** will allow the muscle to develop greater tension for a longer period of time as the muscle tissue increases its **tolerance to lactate**.

See further information in long-term adaptations on page 55.

Lactacid oxygen recovery

High intensity exercise up to about 60 seconds creates **lactic acid**, and **oxygen is needed** to remove this lactic acid. This process begins to restore muscle and liver glycogen, and is relatively slow with **full recovery** taking up to 1 hour (figure 4.6).

Relatively large amounts of lactic acid (15 to 20 times the resting value of 1 to 2 mmol litre⁻¹) are produced during high intensity exercise, which is removed according to the proportions listed in Table 4.1.

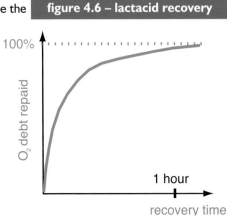

figure 4.5 – phosphagen recovery during interval training

figure 4.6 – lactacid recovery

Removal of the lactic acid

Table 4.1– **removal of the lactic acid**

oxidation into CO_2 + H_2O	65%
conversion into glycogen then stored in muscle and liver (Cori cycle)	20%
conversion into protein	10%
conversion into glucose	5%

The lactate shuttle
During the recovery process after intense exercise, a small proportion of the lactic acid produced is recycled back into glucose in the muscle cell. This is the reverse process to glycolysis and requires energy from ATP breakdown.

Buffering
A **blood buffer** is a chemical substance which resists abrupt changes in hydrogen ion (H^+) concentration. For example, when H^+ concentration increases as a result of intense exercise, H^+ reacts with oxyhaemoglobin (buffer) to form haemoglobinic acid. These ions are released when H^+ concentration falls.

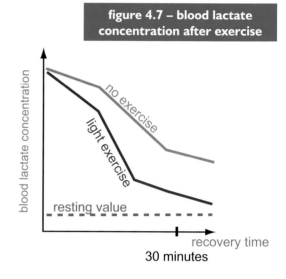

figure 4.7 – blood lactate concentration after exercise

Cool-down following exercise
Cool-down (the process of continuing low level exercise immediately after the end of a high intensity exercise bout) **continues to provide oxygen** to skeletal muscle. This therefore **enhances oxidation of lactic acid** and ensures that less lactic acid remains in tissue. Hence there is less muscle soreness (**less DOMS**).

Figure 4.7 shows how blood lactate falls after exercise, and that when an active cool-down is undertaken less lactate remains in muscle tissue.

Restoration of muscle glycogen stores

* During short duration high intensity exercise, restoration of glycogen takes up to 2 hours, and after prolonged low intensity aerobic exercise, restoration can take days.
* A **high carbohydrate diet** speeds up the glycogen recovery process, and there is a need for the athlete to restore stores as soon as possible after activity, with for example, a high CHO loaded drink immediately following exercise.

Restoration of myoglobin

Muscle myoglobin (an iron protein molecule located in skeletal muscle similar to haemoglobin) serves as a storage site for O_2, and has a temporary but greater affinity for O_2 than haemoglobin. Hence it acts as a **carrier of O_2** from HbO_2 (in blood) to mitochondria (in a muscle cell). Myoglobin is reoxygenated within 2 minutes.

> **STUDENT NOTE**
>
> Restoration of muscle myoglobin is important for recovery from high intensity exercise.

Implications of the recovery process for interval training

When planning training sessions, rates of recovery must be taken into account.
* Recovery between bouts of exercise is dependent on heart rate values.
* As heart rate (HR) falls during recovery, its value is a measure of lactacid recovery.
* Therefore repeating an exercise bout may not be possible until HR has fallen by a certain amount.

Active recovery or cool-down speeds up removal of lactic acid and reduces DOMS.

> **STUDENT NOTE**
>
> **Variance in intensity** of workload in sessions doesn't always stress the lactic acid system, in which case lactate recovery will be much quicker and more complete.

Use of ergogenic aids in recovery

As mentioned on page 40 above, certain ergogenic aids help recovery.

Therapies

- **Physiotherapy**, acupuncture and herbal medicines can be used in injury treatment.
- **Sports massage** is the skilled manipulation of soft tissue for the relief and treatment of muscle soreness and pain, and the maintenance of muscle balance and improved flexilibity. Athletes can benefit from sports massage before, during and after the event.
- **Sports massage** also reduces swelling caused by torn blood vessels, stretches soft tissue, relieves muscle tension, and increases muscle relaxation, hence relieves pain and anxiety. It increases the movement of interstitial fluids that carry away the waste products of fatigue, and stimulates the supply of nutrients such as oxygen and glucose, which speeds up the recovery process. It is often a pleasant experience which prevents injury by dealing with niggles.
- **Acupuncture** is a technique of inserting and manipulating fine filiform needles into specific points on the body to relieve pain or for therapeutic purposes.
- **Ice baths** (figure 4.8) are used to reduce joint and muscle inflammation produced by microtears in tissue created by intense training.

figure 4.8 – are ice baths fun?

These four therapies are used to reduce muscle soreness (**DOMS**) and aid recovery of local damaged tissue.

figure 4.9 – compression clothing as an aid to recovery

Mechanical

- **Specialist clothing** - compression clothing (rubber belts or strapping) to increase hydrostatic pressure within body part.
- Force from the pressure supports the tissue enclosed from the inside, this type of aid reduces injury risk and assists recovery from exercise.
- **Compression clothing** (figure 4.9) also aids venous return and reduces DOMS, hence if used during cool-down will assist recovery.
- **Adidas** are launching (winter 2009/2010) their recovery apparel - **TECHFIT Tuned Compression**. The material is **seamless melted yarn** technology focusing on the highest level of flexible compression on large muscle groups. This is aimed to expel lactate and accelerate **recovery** by up to 5.1%. Zones around the lungs and joints are designed to be flexible, creating garments with comfort and mobility. This is aimed at reducing the necessity for painful ice bath treatment during the recovery process.

Practice questions

1) a) What is muscle fatigue?   2 marks

    b) Describe the possible causes of fatigue during maximal exercise lasting 2 to 10 seconds.   3 marks

2) During intense exercise, athletes can experience a large increase in lactic acid.

    a) Explain the effect of lactic acid build up on muscle function.   4 marks

    b) Suggest strategies that athletes could use to increase their tolerance to lactic acid.   4 marks

    c) Describe the possible causes of fatigue during submaximal exercise lasting between 2 to 4 hours.   4 marks

3) What is meant by the Central Governor Theory and how is it related to fatigue?   4 marks

4) Explain why cool-down is important within an exercise regime.   4 marks

5) a) State where and in what conditions lactic acid is commonly found in relatively large amounts.   2 marks

    b) There are several ways by which lactic acid can be removed from active muscles. Identify the major pathway for the removal of lactic acid and the organs and tissues involved.   4 marks

c)   Identify the **three** other ways, with approximate percentages, in which lactic acid is disposed of in the body.

3 marks

d)   How does light exercise influence lactate removal?

3 marks

6)   Figure 4.10 shows oxygen uptake of an elite games player undertaking exercise followed by a recovery period.

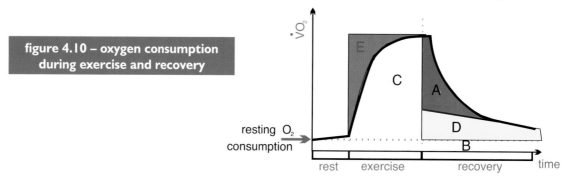

figure 4.10 – oxygen consumption during exercise and recovery

a)   Using the appropriate letters, identify the oxygen deficit and Excess Post-exercise Oxygen Consumption (EPOC).

3 marks

b)   Why does the elite player incur an oxygen deficit during exercise?

2 marks

c)   Excess Post-exercise Oxygen Consumption (EPOC) is considered to have two components. State **two** aims of the first component and explain how this component is achieved.

4 marks

d)   Describe the process of ATP production that restores the oxygen debt or EPOC.

6 marks

e)   Explain why oxygen consumption remains above resting levels after exercise has finished.

3 marks

7)   An elite games player performs an interval training session during which the rate of muscle phosphagen levels during the recovery period was recorded. The results from this training session are given in Table 4.2 below.

Table 4.2 – **muscle phosphagen during recovery**

recovery time / s	muscle phosphagen restored / %
10	10
30	50
60	75
90	87
120	93
150	97
180	99
210	101
240	102

a)   Using the results in Table 4.2, plot a graph of recovery time against the percentage of muscle phosphagen restored.

3 marks

b)   What resting value would you recommend for a full recovery, and what would be the effect of restarting the exercise after 30 seconds?

2 marks

c)   Part of the recovery mechanism after anaerobic exercise involves myoglobin. Explain the function of myoglobin during the recovery process.

3 marks

8)   How could information on oxygen debt recovery be of use to an athlete and coach in designing training sessions?

5 marks

9)   After a particularly strenuous weight training session, a shot putter may experience muscle soreness immediately after the session and the following day. Explain the reasons for this during both these times and identify strategies that could be used to keep the pain to a minimum.

8 marks

10) Recommend a method of optimizing glycogen repletion following hard physical activity.

3 marks

11) Following an intense training session, explain how the following ergogenic aids can assist with the recovery process: having an ice bath, having a massage, wearing full-body compression clothing, and ingesting a hypertonic sports drink.

8 marks

LONG-TERM PREPARATION

Long-term physiological preparation

Key long-term adaptations linked to training methods

Aerobic adaptations

The **aims of training** are to improve performance, skill, game ability, and motor and physical fitness. As mentioned above, **adaptation** refers to **long-term changes** (figure 5.1) produced in the human body which are caused by training overload.

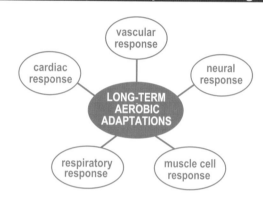

figure 5.1 – adaptations produced by aerobic training

Cardiovascular systems

The cardiovascular system becomes more efficient as the heart becomes bigger and stronger and pumps more blood per pulse. More **haemoglobin** is available in blood for oxygen transport, and the capillary system in a trained muscle bed is utilised better and developed more.

Cardiac response to aerobic exercise

- The heart becomes bigger and stronger (mainly the left ventricle) as a result of prolonged aerobic exercise (figure 5.2), creating **increased ventricular muscle mass** and **stronger elastic recoil** of the myocardium. This is **cardiac hypertrophy**.

- The increased strength of the cardiac muscle causes a more forceful contraction during ventricular systole.

- Therefore stroke volume increases and HR decreases (this is called **bradycardia**), which provides more oxygen per pulse.

- Blood volume increases with training which in turn increases the size of the left ventricular chamber. This means that more blood volume enters the left ventricle per beat (increased **pre-load**) increasing the stretch of the ventricular walls by the Frank-Starling mechanism.

- Reduced systemic vascular resistance (**decreased afterload**) also contributes to the increase in volume of blood pumped from the left ventricle per beat.

- The net effect is up to 20% bigger stroke volume and greater oxygen delivery to muscles.

- Heart rate during the recovery period decreases more rapidly after training.

- Cardiac output at maximal levels of exercise increases considerably and is in a response to an increase in $\dot{V}O_{2max}$. This is because the two components of the cardiac output, namely stroke volume and heart rate, balance each other out and there is an increase in a-$\bar{v}O_{2diff}$ reflecting greater oxygen extraction by the active tissues.

- Cardiac output at rest and at submaximal levels of exercise remains unchanged or decreases slightly after endurance training. Hence there is a **decrease in resting heart rate** (HR) and an **increase in HR during maximal workloads**.

- **Blood vessels in the heart evolve** so that the blood flow to the heart decreases because the heart muscle itself is more efficient.

figure 5.2 – long-term responses of the heart

Trained heart		Untrained heart
120 ml	stroke volume	100 ml
60 bpm	resting heart rate	75 bpm
200 bpm	maximum heart rate	180 bpm

Vascular response to aerobic exercise

The increase in blood flow to muscle is one of the most important factors supporting increased aerobic endurance capacity and performance. This increase is attributable to:

*   An **improved capillary system** – the capillary bed in the muscle system is utilised better and developed, and there is increased capillarisation of trained muscle and improved dilation of existing capillaries due to increase in blood volume.
*   **Diversion of a larger portion of cardiac output** to the active muscle, known as an enhanced vascular shunt. Hence increased vasodilation of blood vessels (such as arterioles) and precapillary sphincters to working muscle.
*   **Increase in blood volume** is attributed to an increase in plasma volume and number of red blood cells. The increase in plasma volume would result in a reduction in fluid friction drag as the blood flows through blood vessels, which would improve circulation and oxygen availability.
*   **Increased elasticity and thickness of smooth muscle** of arterial walls result from extended aerobic exercise which makes arterial walls tougher and therefore less likely to stretch under pressure.
*   Hence blood pressure is maintained (which therefore continues to force blood through the capillary network).
*   Systolic and diastolic **blood pressure decreases** during rest and submaximal exercise. This is because there is a training-induced reduction in sympathetic nervous system hormones. This response decreases peripheral vascular resistance to blood flow, causing blood pressure to drop.

The **net effect** is for the body to develop a more effective blood distribution system both at rest and during exercise.

Respiratory adaptations to aerobic exercise

The respiratory system undergoes the following adaptations to endurance training to maximise its efficiency:

*   Pulmonary systems become more efficient, because the musculature of the torso **becomes stronger** and more efficient.
*   **Lung volumes increase slightly**, hence greater volumes of air can be breathed per breath (known as tidal volume or TV), and per minute (known as minute ventilation or $\dot{V}E$), hence increased gaseous exchange and $\dot{V}O_{2max}$.
*   There is an **increase in vital capacity** at the expense of residual volume, hence a decrease in breathing rate at submaximal workloads.
*   **Maximal pulmonary ventilation** is substantially increased following a period of endurance-based training – compare 100 to 120 dm^3min^{-1} for untrained sedentary subjects with in excess of 200 dm^3min^{-1} for highly trained endurance athletes.
*   Two factors can account for an increase in maximal pulmonary ventilation. These are **increased tidal volume** (TV) and **increased respiratory frequency** (f) during maximal exercise.
*   There is increased capillarisation of alveoli, and more alveoli are utilised, hence increased gaseous exchange and $\dot{V}O_{2max}$.
*   There is an increase in **pulmonary blood flow** (due to increase in stroke volume) and **plasma volume**. This increase in pulmonary driving pressure causes a bigger distortion in red blood cells as they pass through the alveolar capillaries. Hence greater O_2 transfer.

Muscle cell adaptations to aerobic exercise

*   Extended **aerobic exercise** causes **more myoglobin** and more and **bigger mitochondria** to be created in muscle cells, which improves the oxygen delivery and energy creation within a cell.
*   There will also be **increased oxidative enzymes** (such as pyruvate dehydrogenase) produced within muscle cell mitochondria. Hence there will be increased activity of Kreb's cycle and the electron transport chain to restore ATP in muscle cells.
*   Increase in stores and utilisation of **fat**, and increase in stores of **glycogen** in muscle, will enable more fuel to be available for aerobic work.
*   **Glycogen sparing** is a muscle cell response within the specfic muscle cells of the person who has undertaken sustained aerobic training.
*   An adaptation is produced where fats are used earlier on in exercise inside the muscle cells being trained, thus conserving glycogen stores (respiratory factors indicate greater use of fats).
*   The chart in figure 5.3 shows a higher proportion of fats utilised by the trained person, thereby releasing CHO for higher intensity work. This reduces the respiratory exchange ratio (**RER** is a method used in determining which metabolic fuel is predominantly in use during exercise. It is calculated by analysing oxygen comsumption and carbon dioxide production).

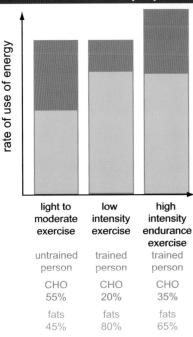

figure 5.3 – contribution of CHO and fats for trained and untrained people

rate of use of energy

light to moderate exercise	low intensity exercise	high intensity endurance exercise
untrained person	trained person	trained person
CHO 55%	CHO 20%	CHO 35%
fats 45%	fats 80%	fats 65%

Further muscle cell adaptations

- There is an increase in a-$\bar{v}$O$_{2diff}$. This is due to a more effective distribution of arterial blood away from inactive tissue to active tissue and an increased ability of active muscle to extract more oxygen.

- A lower mixed venous oxygen content contributes towards the increase in $\dot{V}O_{2max}$ in trained athletes, as observed in figure 5.4.

- Extended aerobic training will initiate conversion of type IIb to type IIa fibres, along with a small increase in the percentage of type I fibres. Hence even better aerobic performance.

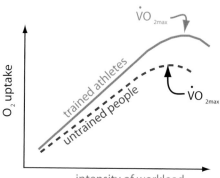

figure 5.4 – oxygen uptake as exercise intensity increases

STUDENT NOTE

You can see from these figures and the diagram (figure 5.4) that $\dot{V}O_{2max}$ is bigger for trained athletes. This is an adaptation produced by aerobic training, which means that the athlete can work harder for longer. Refer to pages 50 and 51 for cardiac, vascular, and respiratory and muscle cell aerobic adaptations.

Oxygen uptake - $\dot{V}O_2$

The amount of oxygen consumed per unit of time (usually 1 minute) is expressed as $\dot{V}O_2$.

Mean value of $\dot{V}O_2$ at rest $= 0.2$ to 0.3 litres min^{-1}.

$\dot{V}O_2$ increases proportionally to work intensity (see figure 5.4) up to a maximum value - called $\dot{V}O_{2max}$.

$\dot{V}O_{2max}$ mean values are:

males (20 yo)	$= 3.5$ litres min^{-1}	
	$= 40$ ml kg^{-1} min^{-1} (for average male body mass 87.5 kg)	
females (20 yo)	$= 2.3$ litres min^{-1}	
	$= 35$ ml kg^{-1} min^{-1} (for mean female body mass 66 kg)	
endurance athletes	$= 4$ to 6 litres min^{-1}	
	$= 75$ ml kg^{-1} min^{-1} (for mean body mass 66 kg)	

Recovery

There is improved oxygen recovery as a result of long-term aerobic training because of **better muscle capillarisation**. If an efficient cool-down is used, **lactic acid removal** is improved, hence reduction in **DOMS** (delayed onset muscle soreness).

Neural response to aerobic exercise

There will be better recruitment of slow twitch fibre motor units making muscle usage more efficient.

OBLA (Onset of Blood Lactate Accumulation)

As **work intensity** increases, **lactic acid** starts to **accumulate** above resting values. At a certain point this produces muscle fatigue and pain, since the resultant low pH (high acidity) inhibits enzyme action and cross bridge formation. This means in turn that muscle action is inhibited and **physical performance deteriorates**.

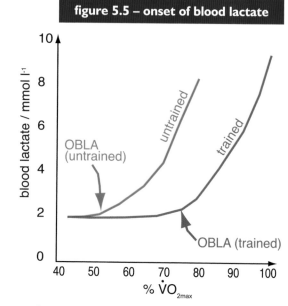

figure 5.5 – onset of blood lactate

This point governs the **lactic aerobic threshold**.

- In the graph (figure 5.5), as exercise intensity increases and $\dot{V}O_2$ increases, untrained people have blood lactate which increases sharply at about 50% of $\dot{V}O_{2max}$.

- But trained athletes can exercise up to 70% of $\dot{V}O_{2max}$ before lactate concentration in the blood increases markedly.

- Hence **trained athletes** begin **OBLA at higher work intensities** - especially since trained athletes have higher values of $\dot{V}O_{2max}$ than untrained people in the first place.

- All this means that the **lactic-aerobic threshold** moves to **higher values of $\dot{V}O_{2max}$**.

Anaerobic adaptations

Changes to the body caused by anaerobic training are listed in figure 5.6.

Muscle cell adaptations (fast twitch muscle fibres)

- **Muscle hypertrophy** (of fast twitch muscle fibres) increases the cross sectional area of existing fibres by increasing (figure 5.7):
  - The number of **myofibrils** within each muscle cell.
  - The **sarcoplasmic** volume.
  - The amount of **contractile proteins**, namely actin and myosin filaments.
  - The **mass** of fast twitch muscle fibres.

- **Hyperplasia** means that:
  - The number of fast twitch muscle fibres increases by the **splitting** of muscle fibres (splitting length-ways), caused by intense exercise as in heavy weight training or plyometrics.
  - Hence the **proportion of type II increases** and the proportion of type I (slow twitch muscles fibres) decreases.

- Increase in muscle cell **stores** such as **ATP**, **PC**, and **glycogen**.
- Increase in **anaerobic enzymes** such as creatine kinase (CK), PFK, GPP, and LDH.
- Increased **toleration of lactate** in fast twitch muscle fibres.
- Improved ability to **remove lactate** from muscle cell into blood, therefore enhancement of alactic/lactate and lactate/aerobic thresholds (a delay in OBLA).
- Hence improved capacities of alactic and lactic acid systems to **resynthesise ATP**, and ability to maintain **maximal power** and **anaerobic capacity** output for longer.
- Decrease in DOMS, particularly following **eccentric training**, such as plyometrics (see page 57 below).

All these adaptations point to an **increase in strength** with prolonged anaerobic training (figure 5.8).

Neural adaptive response

As a result of extended anaerobic training, the following **neuromuscular** adaptations occur:
- Increased **rate of response** of CNS (Central Nervous System).
- **Recruitment** of additional **fast twitch** fibre motor units.
- Improved co-ordination of fast twitch fibre motor units.
- **Toughening of proprioceptors** so that more force is required to stimulate inhibitory signals.
- **Sensory organs** such as **Golgi tendons** (see flexibility section - page 60 below) become **less sensitive** which allows **large muscle forces** to develop in a given muscle which in an untrained person could cause injury.
- Hence a sportsperson will develop **increased strength**.

Changes in structure of the neuromuscular junction

A **neuromuscular junction** lies between a neurone and muscle cell (for details of neuromuscular junctions see page 43 and figure 3.16 of the AS Edexcel Revise PE book, ISBN: 978 1 901424 54 6).

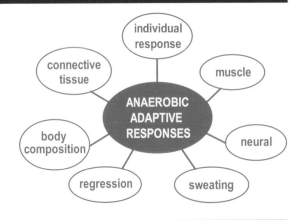

figure 5.6 – adaptations produced by anaerobic training

figure 5.7 – muscle hypertrophy

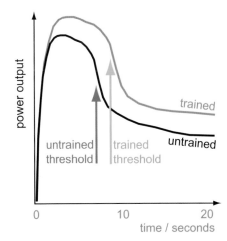

figure 5.8 – comparison of power output for trained and untrained people

The neuromuscular junction

- After prolonged anaerobic exercise, there will be changes in the structure of these junctions within specific motor units (the ones being activated during the high intensity exercise), which will then be related to a muscle's **force producing** capability.
- **Early strength gains** during periods of strength training (between 6 months and 2 years depending on exercise intensity), are almost all due to **increased neural activation**.
- **Long-term strength gains** are mostly due to muscle **hypertrophy**.

Reciprocal innervation

Reciprocal innervation occurs as an **antagonist muscle** is activated less during a movement, hence the **antagonist action is reduced** without conscious effort as a sportsperson performs a powerful movement (using agonists as prime movers). This leads to a small **increase in strength** of the performer in learned and **specific** movements.

Connective tissue response

In response to anaerobic training there will be:
- Increase in thickness and strength of **tendons**.
- Increased flexibility of **ligaments**.
- Thickening and improved **elasticity of cartilage**.
- Improved capability of cartilaginous tissue to absorb and expel synovial fluid (McCutchen's weeping lubrication theory), hence improved **cushioning** against impact within a joint.
- Strengthening of **bone tissue** due to increased depositing of calcium, therefore reduced risk of injury.

Individual response

Adaptive response to anaerobic training depends on the individual:
- **Fitness**.
- **Cultural differences**.
- **Gender**.
- **Psychological** factors.
- **Maturation**.

Sweating as an adaptation to training

As training continues, **heat energy** is produced as a side **product of the metabolic process**, and the need to lose this energy (and avoid heat stroke or hyperthermia) becomes greater. So the sportsperson develops an improved ability to sweat, hence with more efficient heat loss. See page 22 for more on adaptive responses to high temperatures.

Regression

It is a well established principle of training that when training stops, adaptive responses cease. The longer the training the more stable the adaptation produced by the training - the longer the adaptation remains in the person's body and (for example) his or her strength remains high.

Body composition changes due to strength training

Anaerobic training can result in:
- Loss or increase in total body mass (depending on the training regime used and whether male or female).
- **Loss of fat mass**.
- Losses in relative fat (see figure 5.9).
- Gains in fat free mass (FFM).

Females gain much less in FFM than males due to hormonal differences:
- The presence of **testosterone** in males causes an androgenic effect (the building of muscle mass in males).

The **amount of change** of body mass depends on total energy expenditure.

figure 5.9 – body composition changes due to training

can he   become him   with anaerobic training?

Types of training linked to adaptations

The following section deals with how long-term adaptations are produced by different types of training. Figure 5.10 lists these types of training.

figure 5.10 – types of training

Continuous training

This type of training involves continuous activity in which there is **no rest or break** and is normally associated with developing **aerobic capacity** ($\dot{V}O_{2max}$).

The **duration** of the training session should be at least 20 minutes. Adjusting the pace or effort of the activity can vary the exercise intensity (recommended between 60-75% of maximum heart rate) from long, slow distance training to high-intensity endurance training.

Frequency of sessions should be at least 3 times per week to develop aerobic adaptations.

Continuous training almost exclusively develops **aerobic adaptations** as listed above (page 50), particularly development of the oxygen carrying and transport systems of the body, and utilisation of fat stores as a part of the Kreb's cycle stage of aerobic respiration. Long-term continuous training will also **delay the lactate/aerobic threshold**, and will enable the sportsperson to operate at higher lactate levels.

Interval training

Interval training is characterised by periods of **alternating exercise** and **rest**, providing a very versatile training method that enables the individual to perform considerably more work and with greater physiological benefits.

Variables include:
* **Duration** of the exercise period.
* **Intensity** of the exercise period.
* Number of **repetitions** within a set.
* Number of **sets** within a session.
* Duration of the **rest intervals** (rest relief) or recovery.

The exercise **type** and **loading**, number of **repetitions** and **sets**, and length of **rest relief** governs the **adaptive response** produced, thus enabling the individual to select the required intensity of work to stress the relevant energy system:
* **ATP-PC intervals** are characterised by high intensity effort (80-100% of maximum effort) lasting between 3-10 seconds with no more than 2 minutes recovery. This type of training increases ATP-PC stores.
* **Lactic acid intervals** are characterised by medium to high intensity effort (60-80% of maximum effort) lasting between 15-90 seconds with variable recovery depending on exercise duration. This type of training increases blood buffering capacity or lactate tolerance.
* **Aerobic intervals** are characterised by low intensity effort (below 50% of maximum effort) lasting beyond 20 minutes with short recovery. This type of training increases aerobic capacity or $\dot{V}O_{2max}$.

Therefore long-term adaptations to interval training depend on the intensity and duration of the activity.

STUDENT NOTE

You need to review your AS work on Fitness and Training, and Principles of Training. See Chapters 5 and 6 pages 72-90 in AS Revise PE for Edexcel, ISBN: 978 1 901424 54 6.

Periodisation

Periodisation is a method of training which varies training intensity cyclically, organised in periods and cycles of training. Such cycles of training take place long-term, over time spans of months and years.

Each period within a training plan will have a specific aim or objective within the overall training plan, for example:
- Period 1 may be aimed at basic conditioning.
- Period 2 may be aimed at strength development.
- Period 3 may be aimed at speed development.

figure 5.11 – a single periodised year

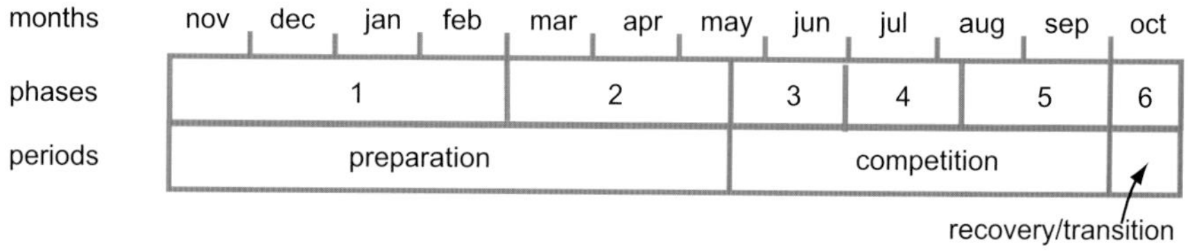

The time intervals within this training method can be defined as follows:
- A **period** is a basic year subdivision between 1 and 6 months.
- A **macrocycle** is a phase lasting between 4 and 26 weeks.
- A **mesocycle** is a phase lasting 2 to 4 weeks which would be part of a macrocycle.
- A **microcycle** is a phase lasting 1 week or less, and is the basic repetitive cycle of activities.

- Sometimes **daily cycles** of up to 3 sessions may be required for elite performers.

months	nov	dec	jan	feb	mar	apr	may	jun	jul	aug	sep	oct
phases	1				2			3	4	5		6
periods	preparation							competition				recovery/transition

Figure 5.11 shows how periods and cycles can be laid out for a whole year. Note that an elite athlete may need a four or five year periodised programme to peak for an Olympic Games.

Planning a periodised training programme
- You will need to utilise the principles of training, decide on general activities, and then decide on specific activities.
- You will need to break down activities into relevance to different energy systems and ensure that this fits the energy system profile for your sport.
- You will next decide on time allocations (**duration**), and decide on the volume of work in a session (**intensity**).

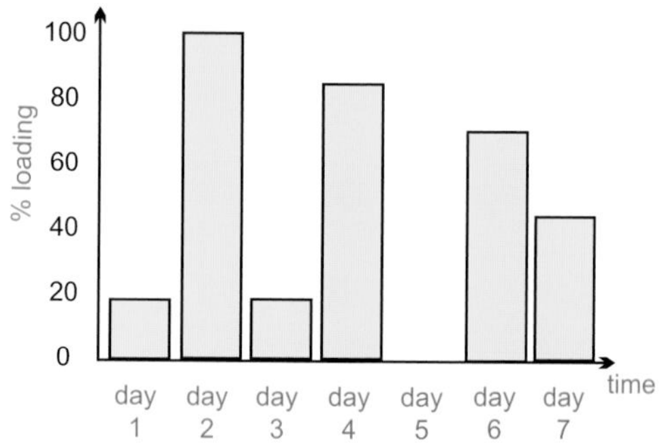

- See figure 5.12 for an example breakdown of training intensity over the days of a microcycle (in this case 7 days long, one week).
- Note that elite athletes who don't need to plan round the working week (most people would have to fit in with school, college or work), often use 5, 6 or 8 day micro cycles to fit in with the time needed to recover from intense training.

figure 5.12 – variation in training intensity during a microcycle

- Decide on how many times in the microcycle you would like to train (**frequency**).
- Set out sets and repetitions within an activity (**repetition**).
- Ensure that **warm-up** and **cool-down** are included.
- Make notes on **progression** for future microcycles.
- Ensure that appropriate rest and **rest relief** is indicated.

figure 5.13 – training intensity by mesocycle

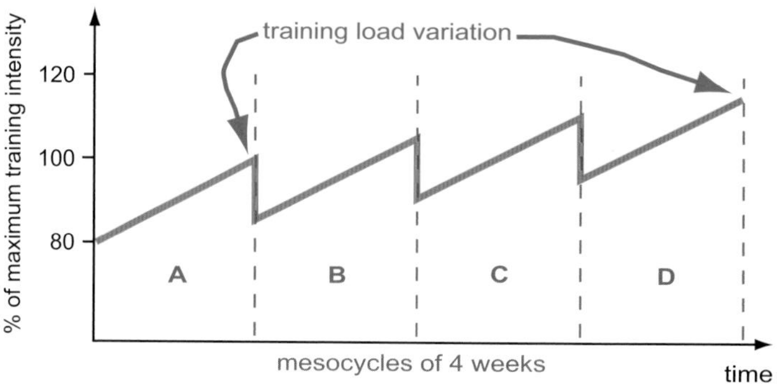

training load variation

mesocycles of 4 weeks

Planning mesocycles
- You need to establish your **maximum training intensity** using fitness tests - this is your initial **100%** training intensity.
- Then decide on a **starting point** below this of, for example, 80%.
- Then plan a **progressive intensity** mesocycle taking you up to 100% in say 4 weeks (see figure 5.13).
- Next plan the subsequent 4-week **cycle** taking you up to 110%.

- With subsequent 4-week cycles taking you up to your planned goal for the year.

Alternative methods of periodisation

- The example in figure 5.11 previously is a single periodised year (just one competitive period). The same sort of arrangements can be made for two competitive periods - called a **double periodised year**.

- Figure 5.14 shows the possible layout for a double periodised year, the blue vertical line shows the end of the first competitive period.

- At this point the second half of the year (period) begins and the process of stucture towards the second competitive period starts. Research has shown that this sort of programme can initiate greater progress in various indicators of fitness (strength, speed, endurance).

figure 5.14 – a double periodised year

months	nov	dec	jan	feb	mar	apr	may	jun	jul	aug	sep	oct
phases	1	2	3	4	5	6	7	8	9
periods	preparation		trans	comp	preparation			trans	comp	

trans = transition   comp = competition   recovery

Tapering and peaking

- The periodisation method of training enables the coach to vary training intensity and quantity, so that a performer can peak for a major games such as the Olympics.
- This peaking usually involves tapering, which means that training intensity gradually reduces over a period of up to 14 days beforehand, which enables the athlete to be fresh and full of energy for the big event.

Peaking is partly psychological. How a performer feels about him or herself, and how confidence is flowing, are often as important as the stage of fitness or strength.

Specialist equipment

Sports equipment manufacturers have developed many specialist training machines **specific** to the sport.
For example:

- Concept II ergo **rower** (figure 5.15).

- **Kayak cross trainer**.
- **Swimming** ergo.
- **Flumes** for rowing, swimming or canoeing.
- **Treadmill** (flat or inclined).
- Spinning **bikes** with varying loads.
- Rollers and standing bikes available for warm-up for track cycling.
- **Resistance training** equipment such as weight training machines or pulley machines (with stacks or hydraulic).

- Towing **sledges** (figure 5.16) or parachutes to increase resistance for running.

Many of these are now designed to **mimic** the sports movement which makes the movement specific to the sport.

figure 5.15 – rowing ergometer

figure 5.16 – sledge resistance

Plyometrics and power training

Power training involves performing exercises with maximum force and speed (**power** is a combination of **force and speed**). The neurological system will be activated at a rate sufficient to produce powerful movements by the muscles being exercised in the sporting situation.

Plyometric training is a type of power training involving **eccentric-to-concentric** actions at 100% effort designed to improve elastic strength.

- Plyometric leg training occurs when, on landing from a jump, the (quadriceps and calf) muscles perform an **eccentric contraction** (lengthen under tension) performed quickly so that the loaded agonist muscle stretches slightly prior to concentric action. This stimulates adaptation within the neuromuscular system, as muscle spindles cause a stretch reflex to produce a more powerful **concentric muscle contraction**. The throwing and catching of medicine balls is a way of developing elastic shoulder strength.

Examples of plyometric training

*   In figure 5.17, two athletes are throwing a medicine ball back and forth. The catch phase of this movement is eccentric for the trunk musculature and the shoulders, with the throw movement being concentric in the same muscle groups.

figure 5.17 – catch and throw as eccentric then concentric exercise – similar to plyometrics

*   In figure 5.18, the athlete is performing two-footed jumping (bunny jumps), which would have to be performed quickly to activate the stretch reflex in time with the concentric phase of the jump.

figure 5.18 – bounding and jumping can be plyometric

The **adaptations** produced by these types of training are almost exclusively **anaerobic**, with muscle strength and hypertrophy as the primary aim. Plyometrics additionally involve neuromuscular adaptations such as the **recruitment** of additional **fast twitch** fibre motor units and improved co-ordination of fast twitch fibre motor units as the eccentric effect is utilised.

For the training to be **most effective**, the greatest force is applied when the **concentric phase** of a movement **coincides** with the **stretch reflex response** occurring at the limit of eccentric stretch.

> **STUDENT NOTE**
>
> Normally, this exercise is done too slowly to activate the stretch reflex, but a rapid rebound movement could have the desired effect.

> **STUDENT NOTE**
>
> Muscle soreness (DOMS) often occurs following plyometric training. This is because of associated damage to muscle tissue and cell membranes (micro tears) and inflammatory reactions within the muscles.

Circuit training

Circuit training is a type of interval training that provides all-round body fitness, characterised by a number of exercises or stations performed in succession so that different body parts are exercised one after the other. The training is normally organised to work for a set time period at each station.

Weight or resistance training

Weight training is a form of **interval training** and can be used to develop or stress several components of fitness such as strength and strength endurance, depending on the **resistance**, number of **repetitions**, **sets** and **rest relief**. Exercises are normally classed in **four** groups:

*   **Shoulders and arms**: bench press, pull downs, curls.
*   **Trunk and back**: back hyperextensions, sit ups.
*   **Legs**: squats, leg press, calf raises.
*   **All-body** exercises: power clean, snatch, dead lift.

Weight training is mostly used for anaerobic adaptations such as **strength development**, involving increased fast twitch muscle fibre recruitment and **muscle hypertrophy**. But it can be used to develop aerobic attributes such as strength endurance.

Speed training

Types of **speed training** include **hollow sprints**, **repetition sprints**, **acceleration sprints** and **resistance sprints** methods, all of which are aimed at anaerobic adaptations (see page 53 above), particularly those enabling neuromuscular developments such as reciprocal innervation. The point of this is to **reduce antagonistic muscles effect** when moving a limb at speed.

Fartlek training

Fartlek or speed play is a form of continuous training during which the **speed** or **intensity** of the activity is **varied** so that both aerobic and anaerobic energy systems and recovery can be stressed.

Core stability training

Core stability training usually uses a number of **different exercises** working the basic trunk muscles:
* Transversus abdominus.
* Obliques.
* Multifidus.
* Quadratus lumborum.
* Erector spinae.

This helps with **basic posture**, and with force transfer from ground to upper body. A lot of exercises use fit-balls (**swiss balls**) or medicine balls, and are usually variations on **basic training movements**.
Adaptations produced will be **neuromuscular** (anaerobic) in nature such that muscles of the torso will be better utilised.

SAQ – speed-agility-quickness training

SAQ involves a number of different exercises which use **agility** as the main theme, with an emphasis on **precision** and **speed** of foot placement. The exercises use ladders or small or large hurdles.

STUDENT NOTE

SAQ is intended to develop the fast twitch motor unit neural firing patterns of the neuromuscular systems to initiate more automatic, explosive movement patterns. Refer to page 44 of 'AS Revise PE for Edexcel' ISBN: 978 1 901424 54 6.

Mobility training – stretching

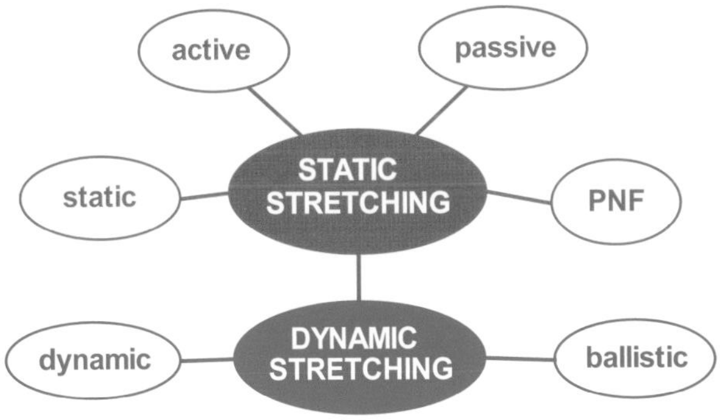

* The aim of mobility training is to improve (or maintain) the **range of motion** over which muscles can act and joints can operate (figure 5.19). In simple language this can be expressed as how far you can reach, bend and turn.
* **Joint flexibility** depends on the distensibility of the joint capsule, adequate warm-up, muscle viscosity and the compliance of ligaments and tendons.
* Flexibility is improved by stressing all these components. The effect produced is based on the **stress-overload** principle by forcing the contractile tissues such as muscle tissue to operate at full stretch.
* Mobility work is best done at the end of an anaerobic training session, during cool-down. This is because the muscular system is usually more relaxed at this time, with muscle temperatures slightly higher than during the warm-up.

figure 5.19 – flexibility/stretching

Types of stretching and flexibility exercises

There are **two** main types of stretching:
* **Static**.
* **Dynamic**.

Static stretching

Static stretching refers to stretching exercises that are performed **without movement**. In other words, the individual gets into a stretch position and **holds** the stretch for a specific amount of time.

Static stretching is performed by placing the body in a position **whereby the muscle to be stretched is under tension**. At this point the position is held to allow the muscle to lengthen. This is a very safe and effective form of stretching with a limited threat of injury. See figure 5.20 as an example of a static stretch.

figure 5.20 – hold this static stretch

Active stretching

Active stretching is **slow stretching** in which flexibility is achieved **without assistance**. This form of stretching involves using only the strength of the opposing muscles (antagonist) to generate a held stretch (held for 10-15 seconds) within the agonist. The contraction of the opposing muscles helps to relax the stretched muscles. See figure 5.21 as an example of an active stretch. Active stretching is a very effective form of conditioning.

figure 5.21 – active stretch

Passive stretching

Passive stretching is similar to static stretching, however a **partner** or **apparatus** can be used to help further stretch the muscles or joints. Figure 5.22 is an example of a passive stretch in which the floor is assisting the position.

figure 5.22 – passive stretch

figure 5.23 – PNF

a

b

c

Proprioceptive Neuromuscular Facilitation (PNF)

PNF is a progression on passive stretching, whereby after a stretch is held, the muscle is contracted **isometrically** for **between 6-10 seconds**. It then **relaxes** and is **contracted** again, usually going further the second time. This is known as the **CRAC** method (Contract-Relax-Antagonist-Contract).

This method is best described in **three** stages:
Stage 1:
*   The athlete and partner assume the position for the stretch (figure 5.23a), then the partner extends the body limb until the muscle is stretched and tension is felt.
Stage 2:
*   The athlete then contracts the stretched muscle isometrically for 5-6 seconds and the partner must inhibit all movement (figure 5.23b).
Stage 3:
*   The muscle group is relaxed, then immediately and cautiously pushed past its normal range of movement (figure 5.23c) for about 6 seconds.

Allow 30 seconds recovery before repeating the procedure 2-4 times.

The aim of PNF is to **toughen** up or inhibit proprioceptors (such as **muscle spindles and Golgi tendons**) in the relaxation of muscle tissue.

This is a long-term adaptation.

Dynamic stretching

Dynamic stretching refers to stretching exercises that are performed with **movement** and are classified depending on the vigorousness of the bounce. Dynamic stretching uses a **controlled**, **soft bounce** or **swinging movement**, that moves a particular body part to the limit of its range of movement and is a preferred method over ballistic stretching.

Ballistic stretching

figure 5.24 – ballistic stretch

- **Ballistic stretching** involves **aggressive**, **dynamic** or **rapid**, **bouncing** or **swinging** movements during which the contraction of the agonist forces the antagonist to relax. Ballistic stretching fails to allow the stretched muscle time to adapt to the stretched position and instead may cause the muscle to tighten up by repeatedly triggering the stretch reflex.

- Ballistic stretching should be **used towards the end of a warm-up** because the muscle temperatures are slightly higher than at the start of the warm-up phase.

- Ballistic stretching is considered to be an outdated form of stretching because of its vigorous nature and risk of muscle tear injury. Activities such as trampolining rely on ballistic stretching during routine work such as a ten-bounce routine. Figure 5.24 shows a side-to-side swinging movement aimed at stretching the lower trunk muscles.

STUDENT NOTE

The force of the contraction should be relevant to the condition of the muscle. For example, if the muscle has been injured, do not apply a maximum contraction.

STUDENT NOTE

Note that the **aim** of stretching training is to initiate anaerobic adaptive changes which involve the neuromuscular system, particularly reciprocal innervation (in which the antagonist action at a joint is inhibited), and **toughening of proprioceptors** so that more force is required to stimulate inhibitory signals. **Sensory organs**, such as Golgi tendons and muscle spindles (within the muscle belly), will become **less sensitive** which would allow **large muscle forces** to develop in a given muscle as a joint is stretched to its limit, which in an untrained person could cause injury.

Practice questions

1) Using practical examples from the cardiovascular systems explain the difference between a short-term response and a long-term adaptation to exercise.   4 marks

2) Identify the long-term adaptations an elite performer would expect to occur to the structure and the functioning of the cardiovascular system, as a result of an intense aerobic training programme.   12 marks

3) Jodie Swallow is a top class female British Triathlete, and has a resting heart rate of 36bpm. Give reasons why such an athlete might have a low resting heart rate.   4 marks

4) Describe and account for some of the long-term effects of regular aerobic training methods on respiratory volumes.   6 marks

5) Describe **four** changes that occur in muscle cells as a result of an endurance-based training programme.   4 marks

6) $\dot{V}O_{2max}$ is the best indicator of cardiovascular endurance capacity and increases substantially in response to long-term endurance training. Define the term $\dot{V}O_{2max}$ and identify its units of measurement. Through what mechanisms does this improvement occur?   8 marks

7) a) The graph in figure 5.25 illustrates neural and hypertrophic adaptations that have occurred in skeletal muscle tissue following 60 weeks of strength training. Explain why early increases in strength are more associated with neural adaptations, but later long-term gains are almost solely the result of muscle hypertrophy.

6 marks

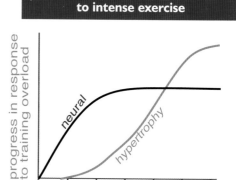

figure 5.25 – anaerobic adaptations to intense exercise

b) What effect would a strength-training programme have on anaerobic capacity and muscle fatigue? 4 marks

c) How could these strength gains be used in the planning of a strength-training schedule for an elite power performer?

3 marks

8) a) Continuous training is one of the least used methods of training by top performers. Identify the **main** characteristics of continuous training and suggest how this can benefit a performer.

4 marks

b) Give reasons why elite performers do not extensively use continuous training as their favoured method. 4 marks

c) Identify alternative training methods used by elite performers and explain why performers favour these alternative methods.

8 marks

9) a) What is meant by the term 'relative training intensity' and in what ways is relative training intensity measured?

3 marks

b) What other factors contribute to the effectiveness of a training programme for an individual sports man or woman?

4 marks

c) Describe an appropriate interval training session for a specific component of fitness in a named sport. 3 marks

d) Discuss the advantages of using interval training in both aerobic and anaerobic training programmes. 3 marks

10) Periodisation is a training concept that explains the variation in training volume and intensity over a specific period of time. Outline the basic structure of a single periodised year and illustrate how a coach is able to use this structure when planning a training programme for an athletics group.

20 marks

11) a) Identify some of the causes of muscle soreness following intense anaerobic training and suggest how it can be prevented.

4 marks

b) What changes might be expected in the lactate threshold as a result of continuous aerobic training? 2 marks

c) In addition to strength work, most physical activities involve the fitness components co-ordination, flexibility and endurance. Give an example of the types of training and adaptive response of the muscle to each of these fitness components.

6 marks

12) Study Table 5.1 which outlines some interval training regimes for the training of different fitness components in a track athlete.

Table 5.1 – **interval training regime**

component	training regime
alactic anaerobic	3 x (10 x 50m)
lactic anaerobic	2 x (3 x 400m)
aerobic	1 x (3 x 1000m)

    a)   Briefly explain the meaning and purpose of the term 'set' in interval training.   4 marks

    b)   What important information is missing from these outline interval training regimes?   3 marks

    c)   Select **two** of the regimes in the table and briefly explain how their particular fitness components respond to such training.   8 marks

13) Fartlek training is a type of training that is used to develop aerobic capacity. What does the term fartlek mean? Illustrate your answer by outlining the training principles used to create a typical fartlek training session.   3 marks

14) a)   Plyometric training is a type of power training, which involves performing exercises with maximum power and speed. Describe the main concepts of plyometric training, illustrating your answer with an example of an exercise. Identify the type of sports performer who would most benefit from this training method.   6 marks

    b)   Discuss the advantages and disadvantages of plyometric training.   4 marks

    c)   Why does muscle soreness (DOMS) often occur following a plyometric training session and how could muscle soreness be reduced?   4 marks

15) Core stability and SAQ training methods are used by most sports performers. Briefly describe these two training methods and the advantages of using these training methods within a general training programme.   6 marks

16) a)   Stretching is a key element in any warm-up. Using an example, identify two **other** elements of a warm-up and explain how they help to prepare an athlete.   4 marks

    b)   Describe **three** different methods of stretching and state a sport that would benefit most from each type.   6 marks

    c)   Identify **two** physiological adaptations to skeletal tissue following a three-month flexibility training programme.   2 marks

17) a)   Give **two** advantages of using static stretching within a flexibility programme.   2 marks

    b)   Identify **two** structural limitations to muscle flexibility.   2 marks

Long-term psychological preparation

Goal setting

Goal setting is the **process of setting targets** to be achieved by a sportsperson in order to aid his or her performance.

The **main function** of goal setting (figure 6.1) is to increase **motivation**. The feeling of satisfaction gained from achieving a goal brings about this motivation. Goal setting can also be used as a means of **managing anxiety** or stress.

Goal setting principles

Goals can be **short**-term, **medium**-term or **long**-term. Short-term goals can be used as targets for single training sessions, or what can be expected after a period of training. Short and medium-term goals are the foundation for long-term achievements. Long-term goals may or may not be achieved, but are placed in the background of a performer's mind and can underpin everything he or she does. Kelly Holmes had the ambition (goal) of getting an Olympic gold, and she **eventually** did this – twice! This goal motivated Kelly to keep going through injury and disappointment, to keep her training through bad weather and good times.

Goals (figure 6.2) should be:
- **Easily attained** initially and therefore **realistic**.
- **Incremental**, a little bit at a time.
- **Challenging** but **achievable**.
- **Progressively** more difficult.
- **Training goals** should be planned around **overall goals**.

figure 6.2 – goals should be?

Goals are either:
- **Outcome oriented**:
  - Towards the **end result** of the sporting activity. For example to win a race.
- **Performance oriented**:
  - **Judged against other performances**. For example to beat his or her best time.
- **Process oriented**:
  - Obtain an improvement in techniques.

Effective goal setting
Goals (figure 6.3) should be:
- Stated **positively**.
- **Specific** to the situation and the performer.
- **Time phased**, to be achieved in 1 week or 2 months for example.
- **Challenging**.
- **Achievable**.
- **Measurable**, so that you can say exactly whether or not a goal has been achieved.
- **Negotiated** between sportsperson and coach.
- **Progressive**, from short-term to long-term.
- **Performance oriented** rather than outcome oriented.
- **Written** down.
- **Reviewed** regularly (with downward adjustment if necessary - in the case of injury).
- **Achievement oriented** rather than failure oriented.

figure 6.3 – effective goals

Failure to achieve goals should be followed by resetting of goals to maintain the performer's **self-esteem**.

S.M.A.R.T.E.R. goals

SPECIFIC

directly related to a sporting situation.

MEASURABLE

progress can be assessed.

ACCEPTED

by both performer and coach.

REALISTIC

challenging but within the capability of performer.

TIME PHASED

a date is set for completion.

EXCITING

inspiring and rewarding to the performer.

RECORDED

written down.

STUDENT NOTE

Remember it is much more easy to set goals than it is to make them work effectively.

Mental preparation

In order to successfully use and achieve goals, the sportsperson will need to implement all the mental rehearsal, focusing and concentration skills discussed in the short-term Section 3.1 above.

It will also be important to be aware of when goals are achieved, and how this mirrors the coach's perception of the current status of a sportsperson's actual performance. This is called **performance profiling** and is usually put into chart form so that discrepancies between performer and coach perception of a performance can be highlighted and discussed. Goals to narrow the gap between perceived and actual performance can then be set.

For example, the chart in figure 6.4 (a wagon wheel or **web chart**) shows the various attributes of a performance, and how performer and coach perceive the achievement of the qualities laid out in the chart. Note that the scores are from 1 to 10 (marked in red on the chart reading outward from the centre of the chart).

STUDENT NOTE

Physiological attributes such as speed, strength, or skill ability are easier to estimate than psychological attributes such as motivation, emotion and so on. Therefore you would expect greater differences between performer and coach perception of psychological performer abilities. This is illustrated by the scores on the web-chart.

From figure 6.4, you can see that the coach's perception of the sportsperson's speed is less than that of the performer himself. Hence, speed training (to improve speed to the coach's expectation) might be a medium-term goal for the performer to set.

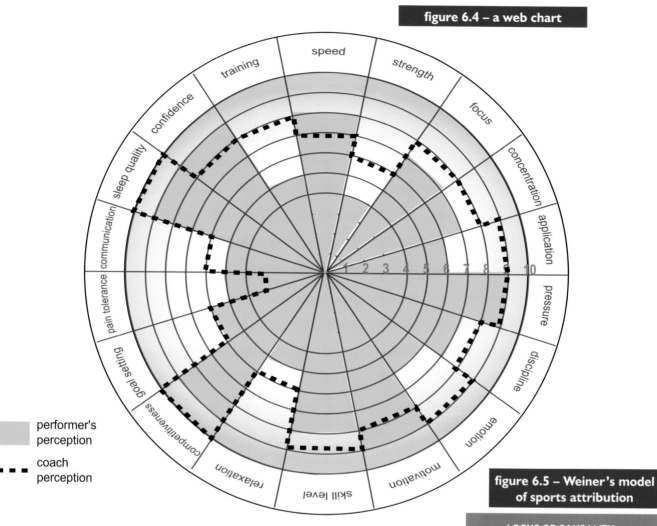

figure 6.4 – a web chart

performer's perception

- - - coach perception

figure 6.5 – Weiner's model of sports attribution

Attribution theory

Attribution is the process of giving **reasons** for behaviour and ascribing **causes** for events. For example, the player played badly today because the weather was poor.

Weiner's model

Weiner's model has four attributions, **ability**, **effort**, **task difficulty** and **luck** (see figure 6.5).

		LOCUS OF CAUSALITY	
		INTERNAL	**EXTERNAL**
STABILITY	**STABLE**	ability 'we were more skilful'	task difficulty 'the opposition are world champions'
	UNSTABLE	effort 'we tried hard'	luck 'the court was slippy'

As in figure 6.5, these attributions are arranged in two dimensions, **locus of causality** and **stability** (with a possible third dimension, **controllability**).

Locus of causality dimension

Locus of causality is the performance outcome caused by:
- **Internal factors** under the control of the performer such as ability and effort.
  - **Ability** is the extent of the performer's capacity to cope with a sporting task.
  - **Effort** refers to the amount of mental and physical effort the performer gives to the task.

- **External factors** beyond the control of the performer such as task difficulty and luck.
  - **Task difficulty** is the term describing the extent of the problems posed by the task including the strength of the opposition.
  - **Luck** describes factors attributable to chance, such as the weather or the state of the pitch.

Stability dimension

Stability refers to the performance outcome caused by stable or unstable factors:

- **Stable** factors are fixed factors which don't change with time such as **ability** or **task difficulty**.
- **Unstable** factors are factors which can vary with time such as **effort** or **luck**.

In attribution theory, **success** is explained by internal attributions, and **failure** is explained by external attributions. **Future expectations** are related to stability. If we attribute success to stable factors, or if we attribute failure to stable factors, then we expect the same next time.

figure 6.6 – Andy Murray
- high achiever

Relationship to sports achievement

- **High achievers** (such as Andy Murray, figure 6.6) tend to attribute **success** to internal factors (such as Andy's incredible state of fitness), and attribute **failure** to external factors (such as the high temperature or strong wind during the match).
- **Low achievers** tend to attribute success to external factors (such as a favourable wind), and attribute failure to internal factors (such as lack of fitness or ability).

- The process of changing attributions is called **attribution retraining**. The point of this is to change a person's tendency to ascribe reasons for success or failure so that it is more like that of a successful performer rather than an unsuccessful performer.
- Attributions affect a sportsperson's **pride**, **satisfaction**, and **expectancy of success**. Some people exhibit **avoidance** tendencies when faced with a sporting situation (they try to avoid participating), and this is called **learned helplessness** (see page 68 below).

Controllability, the third dimension

The **locus of control** covers attributions under the control of the performer (and sometimes not under the control of the performer). The locus of control dimension relates to the intensity of a performer's feelings of **pride** and **satisfaction**, **shame** and **guilt**.

- **Pride** and **satisfaction** are maximised if success is attributed to internal controllable factors such as ability and effort. Then motivation would be enhanced.
- If **success** were attributed to **external** and **uncontrollable** factors such as luck or the fact that the task was very easy, then satisfaction would be less intense and motivation less.
- If **failure** is attributed to internal controllable factors such as **lack of ability** and **lack of effort**, then the overpowering emotion would be dissatisfaction and motivation would be reduced.

The self-serving bias

- This idea crops up because **successful performers** tend to take credit for success. They do this by **attributing success** to their own overwhelmingly outstanding **qualities** (natural ability, **ability** to respond to the competitive situation), thereby enhancing their feelings of pride, self-worth, and self-esteem. They also tend to **blame external factors** for failure.
- Failure is automatically attributed to **avoid internal** controllable and stable factors (even if such factors may be true). This is the **self-serving bias**, people tend to give attributions to **protect their self-esteem** rather than look for true attributions which would reflect the reality of the situation.
- **Unsuccessful performers** do not always attribute failure to external factors and therefore do not protect their self-esteem. This tends to reduce motivation.

Figure 6.7 summarises the attribution process.

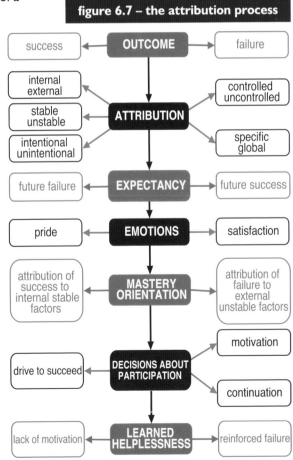

figure 6.7 – the attribution process

Learned helplessness (LH)

As mentioned in figure 6.7, **repeated failure** (or lack of success) can lead to a state known as **learned helplessness**. This is explained as a belief acquired over time that one has no control over events and that failure is inevitable (in figure 6.8, the batsman may feel that he no longer has the skill to succeed at sport). It is characterised by a feeling of **hopelessness** in which a person with the physical potential to achieve highly at sport no longer feels that it is possible for him or her to do so.

figure 6.8 – a batsman fails again!

This is what is behind the common belief that if you fall off a bike, you must get back on straight away, otherwise you may never do so (figure 6.9).

- **General (global) learned helplessness** occurs when a person attributes failure to internal and stable factors, and this feeling of failure is applied to all sports. For example, the comment 'I am useless at all sports'.

- **Specific learned helplessness** occurs when a person attributes difficulties to internal and stable factors, and this feeling is applied to one specific sport. For example, the comment 'I am good at soccer but useless at racquet games'.

figure 6.9 – get back on the bike straight away

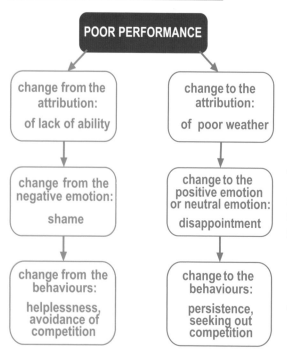

figure 6.10 - attribution retraining

POOR PERFORMANCE

change from the attribution: of lack of ability	change to the attribution: of poor weather
change from the negative emotion: shame	change to the positive emotion or neutral emotion: disappointment
change from the behaviours: helplessness, avoidance of competition	change to the behaviours: persistence, seeking out competition

Attribution retraining

Figure 6.10 summarises the process which must be undertaken if learned helplessness is to be avoided or recovered from. Following failure, low achievers need to learn to attribute success and failure to the same reasons as high achievers, namely:

- Success should be attributable to stable factors.
- Failure should be attributable to unstable factors.

This would raise the **self-efficacy** of the performer for his or her sport.

Motivation

A **motive** is seen as a cause of behaviour which **energises**, **directs** and **sustains** the behaviour. It can be explained as a **drive** to **strive** to meet the needs of the situation in which a person finds him or herself. The strength of such a drive (or motive) depends on the **person** and the **situation**. Different people will have different types and strengths of motives (drives) to meet the needs of the situation. In a sporting context, the term **motivation** implies the driving and striving to **succeed**, to **win**, to **improve performance**, and to **pursue goals** (having set them in the first place).

Intrinsic motivation

Intrinsic motivation (figure 6.11) is the term which describes the **internal** drives or feelings that make us do things.
These feelings come from **within** the performer and involve **enjoyment** of the performance, **satisfaction** of performing, **pride** and the feeling of **well-being** from a job well done.

Extrinsic motivation

Extrinsic motivation describes the feelings coming from rewards **externally** derived (from outside the performer).

These rewards could be **tangible** such as prizes, money, or awards. For example, a gymnastics badge, or wanting to win at basketball because a trophy may be won, or an Olympic medal. Or rewards could be **intangible**, such as approval, praise or recognition from others. For example, attaining a World record initiates praise by the media, initiates national recognition, and reinforces the glory of the situation. Raising social status is a further intangible reward which would reinforce extrinsic motivation.

Arousal

Arousal is a term which describes the level of **inner drives** and which forces the sportsperson to **strive to achieve**. It needs to be **under control** and at the **right level** depending on the task. This striving is linked with the concept of motivation.

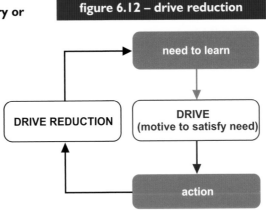

figure 6.11 – motivation

Drive reduction theory

This theory (see figure 6.12) explains why it is sometimes necessary to **vary or renew** the need to learn.

The theory says that the **need to learn** to solve a problem, to learn a skill, or to achieve mastery inspires **motivation**, the **drive** to succeed at the task. This leads to the performer **achieving** the desired outcome (action) which in turn leads to a **reduction in drive** (motivation) to achieve the **same outcome** (since it has already been achieved). This is known as **inhibition**.

The theory explains why people give up sport when it becomes routine, and why changes in for example training venue, training partner, coach or manager, can renew motivation to succeed and continue with a high level of commitment of time and effort.

figure 6.12 – drive reduction

```
need to learn
       │
       ▼
DRIVE REDUCTION  →  DRIVE
                    (motive to satisfy need)
       ▲                   │
       │                   ▼
       └──────────────  action
```

Motivational strategies

These ideas should aim at avoiding or **reducing drive reduction** (reduce **inhibition** of motivation) by changing the **importance** of a task (raise its **status**), or **matching** the task to the performer's needs ('you need to do this to be able to progress towards the Olympic Gold').

Developing and enhancing motivation

Motivation is a combination of personal characteristics and situational aspects.

Motivation is **highest** when:

• The performer is keen to **participate**.
• The performer is keen to **learn**.
• The performer is keen to **perform**.
• The performer is keen to **perform effectively**.
• The motivational **climate** is right.
• The training programme is **interesting** and **varied**.

Enhancing motivation

Motivation is **reduced** by:
- **Routine**.
- **Competition between motives**.

People:
- Have **multiple** motives.
- **Share** motives.
- Have **unique** motivational profiles.
- Need **variation** in **training** and competition.
- Need **variation** in **intensity** and competitiveness.
- Need **structured coaching** and teaching environments.

Motives change over time, and teachers and coaches are important motivators.

Achievement motivation

Achievement motivation is the drive to achieve success for its own sake, and is related to competitiveness, persistence, and striving for perfection.

Achievement motivation is influenced by:
- **Personality** factors, which are:
  - The need to achieve.
  - The need to avoid failure.
- **Situational** factors, which are:
  - Probability of success.
  - Incentive value of success.

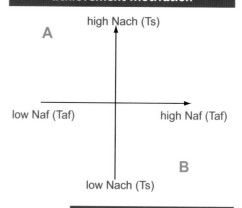

figure 6.13 – personality aspects of achievement motivation

Personality components of achievement motivation
- **The need to achieve (Nach)** or **tendency to approach success (Ts)** personality type likes a challenge, likes feedback, is not afraid of failure and has high task persistence.
- **The need to avoid failure (Naf)** or **tendency to avoid failure (Taf)** personality type avoids challenges, does not take risks, often gives up, and does not want feedback.

The chart in figure 6.13 shows **Nach** against **Naf**, and most people participating in sport will occupy a small region of the chart, for example regions **A** and **B** as shown on the chart.

A = someone with a high need to achieve who will probably have a low need to avoid failure. Such a person will choose difficult or demanding tasks which are more risky, for example, the hard route up a rock face (figure 6.14).

B = someone with a high need to avoid failure who will probably have a low need to achieve, and who will choose tasks which are less risky and more easily achieved. For example, this person will take the easy route up the rock face.

figure 6.14 – high Nach?

Situational factors affecting achievement motivation
The chart in figure 6.15 shows probability of success against incentive value of success, and again most people will occupy a small region (examples here are marked **C** and **D**).

C = region of the chart where a task's **probability of success** is **low** (for example, competing against the world champion), and therefore the sportsperson has to strive very hard to win. The **incentive** to **achieve success** is **very high**, and the sportsperon will be highly chuffed if he or she wins.

D = region of the chart where **probability of success** is **high** (for example, competing in local club match), and the sportsperon therefore doesn't need to try as hard to win. Hence the **incentive to achieve** is **low**, because the person expects to win easily, and of course this is not so pleasing to the performer.

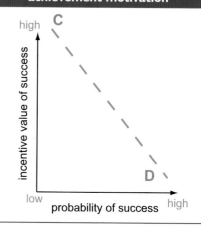

figure 6.15 – situational factors in achievement motivation

What should the coach do?

The prime need for a coach is to improve need and motive to achieve (Nach) in a sportsperson. This is the positive way to deal with motivational issues, and there are strategies he or she could use to **promote Nach**:

* Increase **positive reinforcement** hence increasing pride and satisfaction.
* Ensure that goals are **achievable**.
* Ensure that at least some situations **guarantee success**.
* And subsequently gradually **increase task difficulty** in line with progress.
* Ensure that tasks are **challenging**.
* Ensure that the **probability of success is good**.
* Ensure that the **incentive value of the success is high** (is the race worth winning?).

The coach should also **reduce tendency and motive to avoid failure** (Naf), and this can be done by:

* **Reducing punishment** hence lowering the chance of performer worrying about failure.
* **Focusing negative feedback** on effort rather than ability.
* This avoids the performer tending to believe that causes of failure are internal (due to lack of ability for example).
* And reduces the risk of learned helplessness (see page 68 above).
* **Avoiding** situations where defeat or **failure is inevitable** (such as performing against a much superior opponent).
* If this is not possible **alter the criteria for success** (you will have succeeded if you only lose by 2 goals).

The link between motivation and attribution

Table 6.1 – motivation, attribution and behaviour

	high achiever	low achiever
motivation	high motive to achieve success low motive to avoid failure focuses on pride and on success	low motive to achieve success high motive to avoid failure focuses on shame and worry about failure
attributions	ascribes success to stable internal controllable factors ascribes failure to unstable external uncontrollable factors	ascribes success to unstable external uncontrollable factors ascribes failure to stable internal controllable factors
goals adopted	adopts task oriented goals	adopts outcome oriented goals
task choice	seeks challenging tasks and competitive situations	avoids challenge, seeks very difficult or very easy tasks or competition
performance	performs well in front of evaluative audiences	performs badly in front of evaluative audiences

Skill development and tactics

Visualisation and the use of ritual

Visualisation can be described as the mental or cognitive rehearsal of a skill without actual physical movement. It is used by most top level sportsmen to mentally imagine what a skill or movement is like and how it should be performed. This is often prompted by tape or film or talk from a coach.

Visualisation is used:

* To **review good practice** and compare with poor practice (failure).
* To **rehearse the 'feel'** of a skill before action.
* In **dangerous** situations to avoid risk.
* To **focus** and direct attention.

See page 31 above for details of the **mental rehearsal** process and how it is used. The point here is that visualisation can be used to cement and enhance the learning of difficult skills in order to promote their long-term habituation.

Ritual

Ritual can be a part of the long-term preparation for performance in the context of the establishing of a comfortable and calming routine prior to starting, or for raising awareness of the effort to come, and particularly the arousal level. Most sportspeople will have a routine (then it becomes ritual) warm-up procedure, some will have favourite clothes, shoes or other kit, and some gain ritual confidence from singing, chanting or dancing.

STUDENT NOTE

See page 41 above for some details about ritual, and refer to Hill, Edexcel A2 PE, ISBN: 978 0 435500 60 3, pages 118 to 120.

Training for decision making

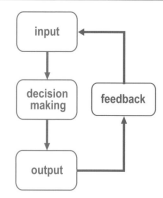

figure 6.16 – decision making

Decision making is an aspect of information processing which can be summarised in figure 6.16. The input in this figure is the information from the surroundings directly via the **senses**:

- **Sight**, **hearing, touch**, **taste** and **smell** (less useful in the sporting situation), which are linked to the various **receptor** sense organs throughout the body.

- **Proprioception** is a term which describes another form of input via the nervous system (sense organs), which relays information to the brain about the position and angles of joints, and the tension in muscles. This allows the sportsperson to be aware of these factors when deciding to make movements.

Perception and attention

Perception is **stimulus identification**. As information is received from the environment, the performer needs to **make sense** of it, to **interpret** it and to **identify** the elements which are **relevant** and **important**. Perception consists of **three** elements (figure 6.17):

- **Detection**, in which the performer needs to be aware that something notable is going on around him or her, where the ball is, where the other players are from both sides in relation to the pitch dimensions, what the goalkeeper is doing, each in a field game situation.

- **Comparison**, in which the performer will compare what is happening with his or her past experiences of similar situations, where are the players in comparison with set plays rehearsed in a training situation?

- **Recognition**, in which the performer realises that what is happening requires a response or an activity in response, what is the response to the rehearsed set play?

figure 6.17 – perception and attention

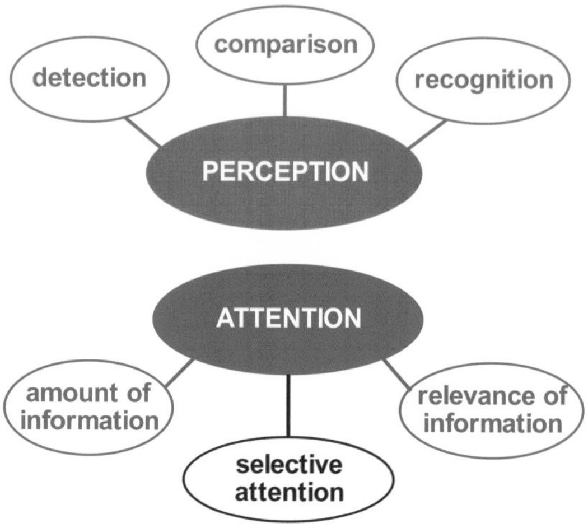

Attention relates to:

- **Amount of information** we can cope with, since the amount of information we can attend to **is limited**, and therefore we have limited **attentional capacity**.

- **Relevance of the information**. The performer must attend to only **relevant information**, and **disregard irrelevant** information. This is called **selective attention**.

Selective attention

This is the process of sorting out **relevant** bits of information from the many which are received. Attention passes the information to the **short-term memory** which gives time for **conscious analysis**. A good performer can **focus totally** on an important aspect of his or her skill which **can exclude other elements** which may also be desirable. Sometimes a performer may desire to concentrate on several different things at once.

When some parts of a performance become **automatic**, the information relevant to those parts does not require attention, and this gives the performer **spare attentional capacity**. This allows the performer to attend to new elements of a skill such as tactics or anticipating the moves of an opponent. The coach will therefore need to help the performer to make best use of spare attentional capacity, and will also need to **direct the attention** of the performer to enable him or her to **concentrate** and reduce the chance of **attentional switching** to irrelevant information or distractions.

Decision making

Having sorted out the input and how relevant bits of information are perceived by the brain, decisions have to be made about what to do. The final part of the equation is the action actually taken - this is the **output**. **Feedback** refers to the fact that the outcome will need to be taken account of as an input before the next decision is made.

An example of how this works is that of a soccer player receiving a pass and then making a pass to another player. He watches the ball arriving (input) and decides to take the ball on his right foot (decision making). He then extends his right foot and attempts to take the ball (output). Depending on the success of his control of the ball (feedback) he then looks up to decide which player to pass to (input again) and decides to pass with his left foot. And so on.
With practice, the decision making can be speeded up as the skill of receiving a ball will adapt the decision to a much simpler and almost automatic brain activity.

Perception dimensions

Figure 6.18 lists the **dimensions of perception** relevant to sporting activity, which relate to the person's ability to be aware via his or her vision processes.

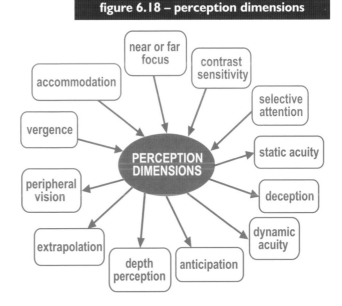

figure 6.18 – perception dimensions

For example:
*   **Peripheral vision** is awareness of movement and images from the edge of the field of vision (out of the corner of the eye).
*   **Depth perception** refers to a person's ability to take in accurate images from both nearby and at distance.
*   **Acuity** refers to the ability to be able to distinguish between nearby objects and sort out the relevant from the irrelevant. **Dynamic acuity** refers to this ability with respect to moving **objects, and static acuity** to stationary objects.
*   **Vergence** is the ability to follow a receding or approaching object.
*   **Contrast sensitivity** refers to the ability to distinguish black and white (and shades of grey).
*   **Accommodation** refers to the ability to focus, by changing the shape of the eye lens (this ability deteriorates in older people leading them to require glasses for nearby viewing).

*   **Anticipation** is a term which describes the process where decisions are made from interpretation of an opponent's movement before a kick, pass or stroke is made, which enables the person to respond more quickly to the opponent's move.
*   **Deception** describes the idea where a sportsperson anticipates that an opponent will try to anticipate his or her own actions - and therefore sends false messages. Hence the opponent's attempted anticipation proves false, and the opponent's move fails.

Improvisation is the skill of sending false or dummy messages prior to a movement in response to an opponent's moves and your movements are not planned or predictable. This makes the opponent's attempted anticipation difficult or impossible.

Rehearsal of skills within a variety of environments and against a variety of opponents can speed up the decision processes. The performer will begin to learn the deceptions and improvisations undertaken by an opponent, which will enable better anticipation of opponent movements.

Memory and decision making

Figure 6.19 (see page 74) outlines the elements of **memory** and how memory contributes to **decision making**.

*   The **short-term sensory store (STSS)** is the **area of the brain** which receives information and holds it for a **short time** (less than 1 second) **prior to processing**. Information deemed unimportant is lost and forgotten and replaced by new information.

The memory process

- **Selective attention** is used to sort out **relevant bits of information** from the many which are received.

- **Short-term memory (STM)** is the **part of the brain** which keeps information for a short period (20-30 seconds) after it has been deemed **worthy of attention**. The STM can carry between 5 and 9 separate items of information which can be improved by chunking (chunking is the process of grouping together a number of similar items for remembering). The information can be used for problem solving (**decision making** in which it is decided what to do) or passed on to the long-term memory for permanent storage.

- **Long-term memory** is the **part of the brain** which retains information for **long periods of time** up to the lifetime of the performer. Very **well-learned information** is stored, and LTM is **limitless** and not forgotten but may require a code for the information to be recalled.

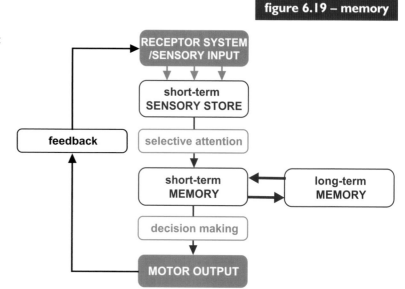

figure 6.19 – memory

RECEPTOR SYSTEM /SENSORY INPUT → short-term SENSORY STORE → selective attention → short-term MEMORY ↔ long-term MEMORY → decision making → MOTOR OUTPUT → feedback

Concentration and cue utilisation

- **Concentration** is a state of mind in which attention is directed towards a specific aim or activity. Concentration and **attentional focus** (control of attention towards a task) are essential components of a sportsperson's armoury of mental techniques to assist performance.

- **Cue utilisation** describes a situation in which cues can be used by the sportsperson to direct attention, and to trigger appropriate arousal responses. This would enable attentional focus at a relevant moment.

- Sometimes, **narrowing of attentional focus** by an aroused player will cause lack of awareness of broader play issues.

- **Cognitive techniques** to assist concentration include imagery, mental rehearsal and relaxation. These methods can be used to direct the sportsperson's mind towards a specific task.

- These techniques can be thought to **manage the stress** of the situation so that anxiety can be dealt with in a productive way.

Nideffer's attentional styles

Nideffer identified **four** styles in which sportspeople can effectively direct attention and enable concentration.

- **Broad,** in which a player concentrates on the whole game, including all players' positions and movements, is best for open skills.

- **Narrow**, in which the player concentrates on one aspect of the game, such as the goalkeeper, is best for closed skills.

- **Internal**, in which the player decides to concentrate on his own technique.

- **External**, in which the player focuses on the position of his opposite number.

Psychological refractory period

The **psychological refractory period (PRP)** concerns what happens when after an **initial stimulus** (which may cause a reaction), there is the presentation of a **second stimulus**. This has the effect of **slowing down** the processing of information causing a **time lag** (this is the **psychological refractory period**) between the relevant stimulus and an appropriate response.

For example, selling a dummy or sidestepping in rugby (figure 6.20).

figure 6.20 – Jason Robinson sidesteps left then right

Example of psychological refractory period

Looking at figure 6.21, time is moving from left to right during the move of a rugby player about to be tackled. **S1** (1st stimulus) would be the dummy. **S2** (2nd stimulus) would be the definite move. If the dummy (**S1**) had been the only stimulus then the reaction would have been at time **R1**. In the meantime, **S2** has happened, but the tackler cannot begin his or her response to this until the full reaction **R1** has been processed by the brain. Hence there is therefore a period of time (the **PRP**) after **S2** before the processing time for **S2** can begin. Once this processing time has begun, there will be a full reaction time period up to **R2** before the tackle can be made. A person who can do a multiple dummy or shimmy (Jason Robinson in figure 6.20) can leave opposition with no time to react and hence miss a tackle.

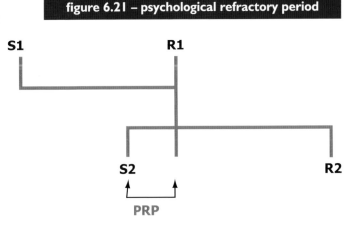

figure 6.21 – psychological refractory period

Group cohesion

A **group** consists of two or more people **interacting** with one another so that each person influences and is influenced by the others. A group will have a **collective identity** and a sense of **shared purpose**, and is a **social aggregate** involving **mutual awareness** and **potential interaction** with structured patterns of **communication**. For examples, a crowd at a soccer match, a soccer team or parents watching their children swim.

Successful groups:
- Have a strong collective identity in which members have an opportunity to **socialise** and who **share goals**, **ambitions** and **ownership** of ideas.
- Will have members who are able to **communicate effectively** (on the same wavelength).
- Will have strong cohesion (see page 76 below).
- Have members who **value relationships** within the group.
- Have a **successful coach** or leader who ensures that **members' contributions** to the group are **valued**.

Steiner's model of a group or team

This model states that:

team success = potential for success - co-ordination and motivation problems.

- **Potential for success** revolves around the issues that usually skilful individuals make the best team, and usually individual success (of team members) correlates with overall team success.
- **Co-ordination problems** (for players) occur if there should be a high level of interaction between players, but one (or more) player is being selfish or aggressive, or if a defence is not working together, and hence overall team performance suffers.
- **Motivation problems** occur because people seem to work less hard in a group than they do on their own. For example, in rowing, times of winning double sculls are often only slightly faster than single sculls. This is **social loafing**, 'the **Ringlemann Effect**.'
- **Motivational losses** occur because individuals may not share the same motives. This leads to loss of group cohesion, for example, some players may play a game for social reasons, others in order to win.

Social loafing, the Ringlemann Effect

- **Social loafing** is the term which describes the fact that individuals appear to **reduce their effort** when in a group (figure 6.22), and can **hide their lack of effort** amongst the effort of other group members.
- It can be eliminated if the contribution of an individual **can be identified** as with **player statistics** (American football, rugby league, cricket, basketball).
- The **need** for interaction between players varies between sports.
- **Co-operation** between players can be significant in eliminating social loafing.

figure 6.22 – social loafing

Cohesion

Cohesion points at the way in which group members **gel** together, or feel **collective affection** for one another, or feel a strong **sense of sharing** whatever it is that the group does. It is the extent to which members of a group exhibit a desire to **achieve common goals** and **group identity**.

* Sometimes this can mean selection of less skilled but more co-operative players for a team.
* Unfortunately, friendship groups can have negative effects.

Cohesion has both **task** and **social** elements:

* **Task cohesion** is about people who are willing to work together (figure 6.23) whether or not they get on personally, hence the group would have the potential to be successful.
* **Social cohesion covers the notion that** teams with high social cohesion but low task cohesion are less successful.

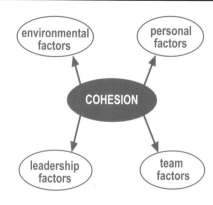

figure 6.23 – cohesion is important for some teams

Carron's model

This model (figure 6.24) outlines **four** factors that affect the development of cohesion:

* **Environmental factors** which bind members to a team, for example, contracts, location, age, eligibility. To make cohesion stronger, you should avoid a star system and provide opportunities for socialising.
* **Personal factors** which feature things that members believe are important, and include motives for taking part. To optimise on cohesion, a coach should give opportunities for motives to be realised, and develop ownership feelings and social groupings within the team.
* **Leadership factors** which are about the behaviour of leaders and coaches. Coaches should use all leadership behaviours to influence different individuals.
* **Team factors** relating to the group, including team identity, targets, member ability and role, creation of team short- and long-term goals, and the rewarding of individual and team efforts.

figure 6.24 – Carron's model of cohesion

environmental factors

personal factors

COHESION

leadership factors

team factors

Practice questions

1) a) Show what is meant by short-term goals and long-term goals by using examples from sport. 4 marks

b) What are the main positive effects of setting goals in sport? 2 marks

c) As a coach how would you ensure that your goal setting was as effective as possible? 6 marks

d) How does performance profiling assist in goal setting? 3 marks

2) Explain the meaning of the acronym S.M.A.R.T.E.R. in relation to goal setting. 7 marks

3) a) Figure 6.25 partly illustrates Weiner's model of attribution. Explain the term attribution using a sporting situation. 2 marks

b) Explain the terms locus of causality and stability when applied to attribution theory. 4 marks

c) Redraw the model and place on it relevant attributions for each of the four boxes. 4 marks

d) What attributions would you encourage if your team were playing well but often losing? 5 marks

figure 6.25 – Weiner's model of attribution

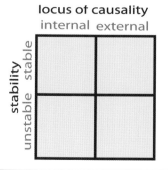

locus of causality
internal external

stability
stable
unstable

4) Those who achieve little in sport often attribute their failure to factors outside their control and learned helplessness can result. Using examples from sport, explain what is meant by learned helplessness and identify how self-motivational techniques may help to limit the effects of learned helplessness. **6 marks**

5) A number of elite athletes are attending trials at their chosen sport. Describe the Inverted U theory and explain how it might affect their performances at the trials. **5 marks**

6) The catastrophe theory is used to explain a golfer's disastrous failure to win a match having been 3 strokes in the lead coming up to the last green. Explain this situation and why this theory might be useful in preventing a repetition. **4 marks**

7) a) Describe the characteristics of the positive motive 'the need to achieve'. **4 marks**

   b) Describe an example from sport of someone who has a high motive to avoid failure. **I mark**

   c) Identify factors that could affect the use of motives to achieve and to avoid failure in sporting situations. **3 marks**

   d) How would you promote the 'need to achieve' motive, rather than the 'need to avoid failure' motive? **8 marks**

8) a) What is meant by intrinsic and extrinsic motivation? Give practical examples to illustrate your answer. **4 marks**

   b) How can extrinsic motives affect intrinsic motivation? **2 marks**

9) a) A top tennis player wins Wimbledon twice, but then in spite of being uninjured finds it difficult to get beyond the initial stages the following year. Explain this loss of motivation. **4 marks**

   b) The training seems harder, the effort doesn't seem worth it to try again. Suggest **two** strategies a coach might use to re-motivate the player. **2 marks**

10) a) Identify the three main receptor systems used by a performer in sport. **3 marks**

    b) Where is the filtering mechanism found in an information processing model? Explain what happens with information as it passes through this mechanism. **2 marks**

11) a) Using figure 6.26, which represents the human motor control mechanism, state what is meant by short-term memory and long-term memory. **2 marks**

    b) How can information be retained in the long-term memory? **4 marks**

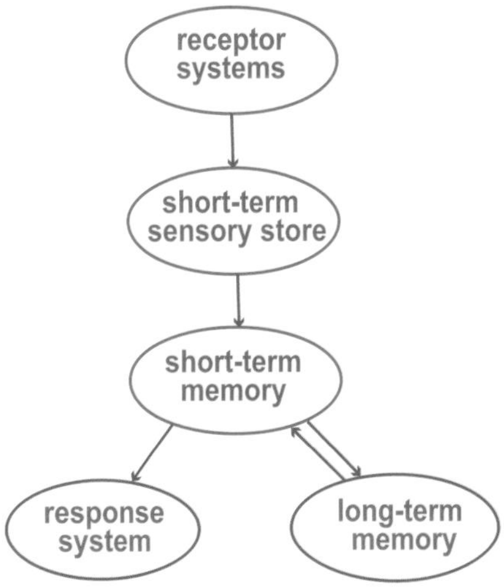

12) a) Using the example of a table tennis player receiving a serve, what information would be held in the short-term sensory store, and for how long? **2 marks**

    b) Name and describe the purpose of the process by which information is transferred from the short-term sensory store to the short-term memory. **4 marks**

    c) What types of information would you use (if you were a table tennis player receiving a serve) from your short-term memory? **3 marks**

    d) What types of information would you use (if you were a table tennis player receiving a serve) from your long-term memory? **3 marks**

figure 6.26 – the human motor control mechanism

13) a)   What is meant by cohesion in the context of teams?   4 marks

   b)   What factors stop a team ever performing to its true potential?   6 marks

14) a)   Explain what is meant by social loafing by using examples from sport.   3 marks

   b)   What advice would you give a team coach to ensure maximum productivity?   5 marks

Long-term technical preparation

Mechanical

Refinement of technique

figure 7.1 – Rebecca Romero multi-sport superstar

Technique amounts to the sequence of actions necessary to perform a physical skill **accurately** and **efficiently**, and will depend on:

* The **physique** and **strength** of the performer.
* The **requirements** of the sport or skill.
* The **mechanics** of the desired movement.

It is also important to note that technique is **highly specific** to a sport or activity (sometimes to a group of related activities such as racket sports). This means that an expert performer at one sport (for example cycling or cricket) may be absolutely useless at another sport (in the same example, swimming). It may be possible for such a performer to learn a new technique for a different sport, but examples of this are rare.

An example of a person who has been able to transfer to a different sport from an elite level at her first sport is **Rebecca Romero**, silver medallist in rowing at the Athens Olympics 2004, and gold medallist in cycling at the Beijing Olympics 2008 (figure 7.1). Rowing and cycling have similar cardiovascular requirements but vastly different technical requirements.

figure 7.2 – an early learner of technique

* Learning a successful technique is a **long-term process**, starting from basic skills specific to a sport or athletic event (figure 7.2), then making adjustments as the perfomer learns how to perform.
* This is a complex matter because a young performer will **observe** others and will attempt to **imitate** them whether or not the technique being observed is correct.
* This depends on the **status of the role model** (whose technique is being copied), and the **complexity of the task**.
* Most young people will arrive at their first training session for a popular sport with some idea of the skill of the sport.
* Coaches like to start from scratch when it comes to teaching technique. This is rarely possible.

Refinement of technique involves:
* Knowledge of the **perfect technical model** by a coach.
* Knowledge of the **mechanics** of a skill.
* Being aware of methods by which technique can be **changed**.

Hence, **refinement of technique** refers to the fine-tuning of the sequences of movement which will lead to the perfect technical model.

Observational feedback is the process whereby the coach will decide what changes to technique need to be made based on the **comparison** between the performer and the perfect model. Hence the **amendments** necessary will need to be explained to the perfomer. Sometimes these changes will be very small but could make all the difference between a good performance and a very good performance.

The first step is to observe the performance by **video analysis**, and **compare** this with an excellent technical model (based on an elite performer).

Video analysis

Apart from the simple digital camera, there are many software systems which analyse and compare technique. Some of these look at body positions, angles and speeds (the body is represented by a series of straight lines, see figure 7.3).

Examples are:
* Motionview.
* Quintic.
* Dartfish.

figure 7.3 – examples of software analysis

These systems also provide frame to frame comparison between the performer and a technical model (figure 7.4).

Positional software

Other systems look at the movement of players during a game.

Prozone uses up to 12 fixed cameras and sensors around a pitch or playing area. This analyses the positions and speeds of players at up to 10 times per second (10 Hertz), which enables a coach or manager to analyse the strategy and tactics within a game. In 2009, 14 premiership soccer clubs used the system to serve up such factors as:
* Average player recovery times.
* Number of high intensity activities (speed > 5.5 ms^{-1}).
* Average total distance per team match.
* Marking and off the ball play of individual players.

figure 7.4 – technique comparison software

The first three of these factors are **fitness indicators** (as opposed to technique analysis), and the fourth has bearings on **strategy and tactics.**

Comparison between premiership and championship soccer teams shows a range of factors which the championship sector can then attempt to improve to the premiership level on the basis that if they match the premiership indicators, they will be able to gain promotion!

GPS applications

A **GPS** (global positioning system) device contains a small receiver chip that links to an array of satellites orbiting the Earth to give position and speed of an object.

* Yachting and sailing use GPS to assist navigation. This is a long standing application.

* A soccer ball is being developed which will contain a GPS system chip, which will be able to ascertain whether or not the ball is out of play, or over the line in the goal, and therefore scoring. Again, this is by real-time feedback to a central computer which would enable the fourth official to make a sensible decision.

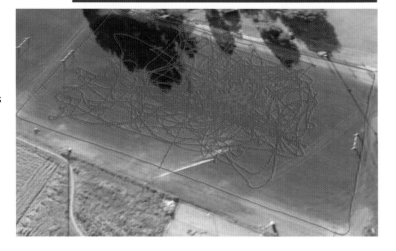

figure 7.5 – GPSports dataplot of a single player

* **GPSports** have developed a system in which a device carried (strapped to the torso) by a player is monitored for position by GPS technology (and also monitors heart rate). The position (in 3D if necessary) is then communicated to a pitchside computer via wireless transmission. Some sports allow the devices to be worn during competitive games (for example, hockey). The output is of the form shown in figure 7.5, which is a dataplot overlaid on a Google-Earth image of a single player during a soccer training match. Further data include speeds and distances run of single players which can be used in a similar way to Prozone.

- GPS data can be linked to programmes such as Google Earth to create simulation of course terrain. For example, cyclists can ride a course without actually being there. Race plans can be prepared from this visualisation process. Indoor GPS applications include links to heart rate monitors and even video to gain a better picture of an athlete's performance.

- As with any technology, accuracy of data is sometimes questionable and cost is a major issue.

Technical ergogenic aids

These are devices used to analyse technique and the mechanics of a movement, or monitor essential factors of a performer's activity.

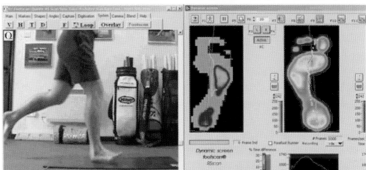

figure 7.6 – Quintic force plate analysis

Force plates
- A **force plate** is inserted into the ground at the take-off area for a long jump or high jump, or in the space in a track immediately after a sprint start. This enables the patterns of force (figure 7.6) made by a foot striking the plate to be determined.
- This information (combined with video of the same footfall) can tell a coach the precise way in which the foot is active during its strike with the ground, and enables him or her to assess whether **changes in foot posture** are required.

figure 7.7 – a pedometer

Pedometer
- A **pedometer** is a wrist worn device (figure 7.7) used to detect footfall.
- What a pedometer actually detects is the **impact** between foot and the ground, which causes the whole body to decelerate and accelerate.
- Therefore it is an **inertial device** detecting change in position, and its purpose is to count the number of footfalls during a race, training session or activity.
- A coach will use this information to assess **stride length** or total energy output.

Heart rate monitor
- The **HR monitor** is fairly old technology, which can be strapped to the torso or worn as a watch-like device on the wrist (figure 7.8).
- Heart rate can be observed by the performer during training or competition to ensure that HR operates within a predetermined training zone (see AS Revise PE for Edexcel, by Jan Roscoe Publications, ISBN: 978 1 901424 54 6, page 85).

This technology works by detecting the electrical signal produced by the heart during its beat similar to ECG technology. It allows the performer to predetermine and maintain the training intensity throughout a session.

figure 7.8 – a HR monitor

Loughborough University Sports Technology Institute
Loughborough University have a Sports Technology Institute, examples of whose tasks include:

- Reassessing how **footwear** can be made to match the **shape and mechanics** of feet on an individual basis (figure 7.9). The foot is scanned to capture its shape, then footfall is analysed (using forceplate technology). This indicates exactly how the foot lands and moves, and leads to the construction of personalised footwear, whose aim is to make movement more efficient and improve performance.

- Attempting to determine the correct **angle of entry** of a swim start dive to ensure maximum start speed.

- Introducing the **RespiVest**, a close fitting corset-like vest, which constricts breathing, and stresses the breathing system. This is an overload on the respiratory musculature, and means that the performer will be able to breathe more efficiently when competing (without the vest!).

figure 7.9 – Dan Hipkiss - with specially moulded shoes

Drag and swimsuits

The new sharksuits which have reduced swim times by between 1 and 5%, and which have now been banned for the 2010 season, were developed by analysing the shape and material using computer simulation and analysis from wind/fluid tunnel results.

Wind tunnels

Wind tunnels within University Sports Science departments are increasingly being used to assess the aerodynamics (improved flow of fluid - air or water - reducing drag or fluid friction) of bikes, cycle helmets, and cyclist overall profile. This is done by blasting air past the stationary object in a tunnel, and using smoke to illustrate the layers of flow of the air. The task is to avoid vortex generation in the air flow, since smooth (laminar) flow generates less drag.

Factors investigated include:
*   Wheel spokes and profiles.
*   Width of handlebars.
*   Riding posture.
*   Type of cloth and design of clothing.
*   Hand position on the bars.
*   Forward cross-sectional area of frame and brackets.

> **STUDENT NOTE**
>
> See pages 38 and 47 above for some details about clothing in the context of mechanical ergogenic aids.

Technology and drag

The computer programmes show how adjustments to shape can be made **before** construction, reducing expense and making more systematic the shape-making process. In addition to the cycling applications above, this is for:
*   Kayaking and rowing.
*   Bobsleigh, luge and skeleton.
*   Speed skating (helmets, costumes and body angles).

Further application of the same technology is to **increase the drag effect** in order to improve propulsion in water-based activities. This applies to:
*   Improved patterns of pulling (hand and foot/leg positions and activity) in swimming.
*   Shape of blades in rowing/canoeing.

Future developments in technology

The electronics will continue to be developed for existing technologies. For example, performers using a treadmill will be able to have gas analysis, heart rate monitoring, gait analysis, and suggested training programmes produced as a result of a single session.

Kit and equipment
*   The most obvious development in athletic clothing will be a **single composite fibre** that does everything currently achieved by a range of materials.
*   It would need to be **stretchy**, **light** and **steel-tough** that **wicks** away sweat, **insulates** in such a manner as to maintain a constant body temperature, is **rainproof**, and perhaps **fireproof**.
*   For protective ski clothing and sports such as motor racing there is the potentially revolutionary **d3o** – a shear-thickening material in a soft foam base.
*   Its shear-thickening property means that the greater the force acting on it, the more **solid** the material becomes.
*   On impact it suddenly hardens to provide instant **armour** without padding.
*   For more information on d3o try: http://d3olab.com.

*   New **faster start blocks** for swimming will be in use in international competition in 2010.

Racket design
*   Cutting edge development in racket design includes the incorporation of **piezoelectric crystals** into the frame, which produce electricity under stress.
*   The current generated by a ball hitting the strings is amplified and returned to the crystals in the frame, causing the frame to **stiffen** to give greater power and 50% less vibration.

Footwear design
* The shoes of the future will be even more **sport-specific** than they are now.
* With football boots, the aim must be to let the players feel as if they are playing in **bare feet**.
* Such shoes would contain some form of **shear-thickening** material where ball contact is made.
* Support and **grip** might be met with **intelligent fabrics** and materials.
* And sole grips that self-adjust to the requirements of the **pitch** and conditions.
* **Cushioning** will improve so that the incident of hairline fractures reduces.
* **Self-cleaning** shoes goes without saying.

Protective clothing
* The **safety helme**t of the future will be wholly breathable, far less bulky thanks to d3o-type materials, packed with microchip technology and personalised by the wearer.

Environmental conditions
What about playing in all light conditions?
* Currently cricketers wear sunglasses that cut out ultraviolet (UV) rays, glare (polaroid lenses) and enhance the light in dark conditions.
* These lenses get dirty and can only be used in slow-moving sports. The answer would be to develop a form of contact lens that does everything done by sunglasses.

Stadia of the future
* The 2012 Olympic stadium in London is currently being built with the latest technological specifications.
* Tokyo's unsuccessful bid for the 2016 Olympic Games and their marketing strategy was to provide a central sporting complex that had a negative carbon footprint.

* The concept of millions of people traipsing across the World for global entertainment, leaving an enormous green footprint, may be unacceptable in years to come.
* The online digital alternative may be the solution!

* The concept of a Sports Village has been realised at Stirling's new training and competition base offering swimming pools, ice rink, games hall, gym, climbing wall and 3G pitches.

Practice questions

1) What does 'refinement of technique' mean to sports performers?   2 marks

2) How do the following technologies aid analysis and feedback for improvements in sporting performance?   12 marks

    a)   Video and computer software analysis.
    b)   Heart rate monitor.
    c)   3D scanning machine.
    d)   Force plate technology.

3) Wind tunnel technology is increasingly being used to assess the aerodynamics of sports equipment. How has this technology influenced the success of teams such as the Great Britain cycling squad?   5 marks

4) Discuss the notion that sports performers are only as good as the technology that supports them. Use examples from global sports to support your answer.   20 marks

5) Comment on how the future of sport may be affected by the developments in technology. Illustrate your answer with examples.   12 marks

MANAGING ELITE PERFORMANCE

CHAPTER 8
CENTRES OF EXCELLENCE

CHAPTER 9
TECHNICAL SUPPORT

CHAPTER 8: *Centres of excellence*

STUDENT NOTE

The focus of this section of the syllabus is on **elite performers** throughout the World. It involves the study of **sports excellence** in a socio-cultural context, starting with the historical development of elite sport from the beginnings of pedestrianism and the prize ring, to the emergence of **amateurism** in the 19th century, and the growth of **World competition** in the second half of the 20th century. Four countries are picked out to illustrate this process, **East Germany**, **Australia**, the **USA** and the **United Kingdom**, culminating in the acceptance of **professionalism** in the Olympic Movement.

The historical development of elite sport

The focus of **popular recreation** is normally centred on the **lower classes**, **aristocratic** or **gentry** sports co-existed alongside peasant sports. Normally, **patronage** by the gentry not only determined whether the popular activities and **festivals** flourished in a community, but it was also why they were allowed to continue well after levels of industrialisation and urbanisation had increased. Figure 8.1 summarises the characteristics of popular sport in Britain before the 18th century.

figure 8.1 – characteristics of popular sport

occasional · wagering · local · violent · POPULAR SPORTS · peasantry · ritual · rural · uncodified

The key factors were:
* The significance of **wagering**.
* The **limited free time** available to the urban lower class and agricultural labourers.
* The **minimal pay** for workers who were on the bread-line.
* The **lack of transport** except for the wealthiest classes.

As a result, the **occasional festival** and fair offered the chance to **earn money prizes** through sporting competition to young people with talent and bravery. If they were good enough, they could increase their income by travelling to different fairs and wakes to compete in combat sports like single stick play and wrestling or running events. In addition to prize money, there was always **wagering** where you could risk money on backing yourself to win or lose!

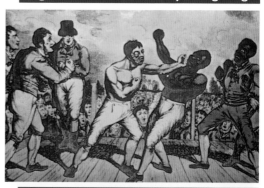
figure 8.2 – bareknuckle prizefighting

The prize fighter and the pedestrian

Prize fighting and **pedestrianism** are chosen because both involved professional performers by the end of the 18th century, both had the opportunity to win large sums of money, and both involved the upper class and the peasantry in a partnership in which high standards were achieved.

Prize fighting
Prize fighting (figure 8.2) dates back to the 13th century when there were gladiatorial schools, relics of the Roman Conquest, where individuals were prepared to defend themselves and compete in 'sword and buckle' contests. By the time of the Tudors, there were so-called professors of defence, who formed a company called **Masters of Defence**. This was the cradle of the **Noble Art of Self Defence**, which came to prominence in the 18th century with **James Figg** opening the **Academy of Boxing** in

figure 8.3 – Figg and Broughton

London in 1718. As a Master of Defence one had to be able to defend oneself against all-comers at swordplay, cudgels, quarter staff and grappling. He would also be employed as a tutor to fashionable young 'dandies' and aggressive 'dualists'.

When **Jack Broughton** (figure 8.3) became champion, he changed the rules of the prize ring to establish **pugilism**, limiting the contest to **bare-knuckle** punching and throws. The tradition of teaching the gentry resulted in '**sparring**' being developed and '**mufflers**' (the precursor of modern boxing gloves) for protection.

Wagering

With **wagering** taking place, there was always an element of **corruption**, and when the Duke of Cumberland lost heavily because Broughton was unexpectedly beaten by Jack Slack, he used his influence to drive the sport underground. From this time, the 'Fancy' had to run the gauntlet of police and magistrates. Right through to the 1830s **huge crowds** were attracted to major fights and fortunes were won and lost.

Pedestrianism

The term **pedestrianism** referred to a group of mainly lower class individuals who earned part of their living by competing in certain sports **for money**. It was a forerunner of the term **professional**. One of the earliest examples of this was racing 'wager boats'. The most famous example was the Doggett Coat and Badge event involving Thames watermen coming out of apprenticeship (an early winner of which was Jack Broughton, pugilist).

However, the most popular use of the term existed **on the roads** where the upper class used **footmen** on their coaches and these took part in **wager foot races**. These races eventually developed into **challenge events** over **long distances**, with **wagers** being made on the result or on the 'walker' completing a self-imposed task successfully.

Wagering

One of the most notorious occasions of this type occurred in 1800, when **Captain Barclay** completed 1000 miles in 1000 hours. There was so much money to be won that wealthier athletic young men took up these challenges, although many events had a circus element and were open to **corruption**. Even though amateur sport was emerging, these professional contests continued well into the 1870s with an American athlete, **Edward Payson Weston**, coming to England and completing 2,000 miles in 2,000 hours around England and giving a talk on 'abstinence' each evening. Another great American professional athlete, **Deerfoot**, came to England, prepared to take on all-comers in races from one to ten miles. When he ran out of challengers, he was encouraged by 'punters' to debase his skills by competing against **horses** and **cyclists**.

figure 8.4 – gentleman v pedestrian

- As with the prize ring, pedestrianism **attracted huge crowds**.
- There was a great deal of **wagering** at each stage of the race. The gentry were only too prepared to bet on men as well as horses at this time.
- The professional walkers and runners were managed by businessmen and considerable **commercialism** was involved.
- The **gentry** were also willing to test themselves by **competing against a pedestrian** in public arenas (figure 8.4).
- This marked the age of the **Corinthian gentlemen**, prior to the emergence of public school athleticism.

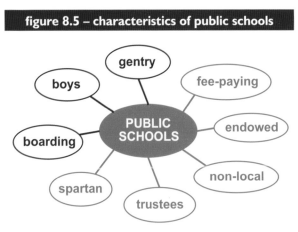

Excellence

There are **two** separate notions of **excellence** within these developments:
- The **talented individual** (from a peasant background) managed to compete in festivals and win prizes, but this tended to be occasional as work and survival came first.
- There was a **professional elite**, whose talent was such that they could earn a good living through challenge events and **wagering** successfully.

Elite performance and 19th century public school athleticism

STUDENT NOTE

The second phase in the development of elite sport in England occurred in **19th century boys public schools**. This development was summarised in the book 'AS Revise PE for Edexcel, ISBN: 978 1 901424 54 6', Chapter 8 Section 1.2 and should be an automatic part of revision for this section of the A2 Syllabus. The following notes amplify and clarify the AS summary.

Figure 8.5 outlines the characteristics of the public schools.

figure 8.5 – characteristics of public schools

gentry, boys, fee-paying, endowed, PUBLIC SCHOOLS, boarding, non-local, spartan, trustees

The public schools

The clearest definition of '**the public school**' in England from around 1800 is:

- An endowed place of education of old standing to which the sons of gentlemen resort in considerable numbers, and where they reside from eight or nine to eighteen years of age.

The age 9 to 18 is the formative period for boys with the advantage of attending a public school, when sporting talent will develop if encouraged. So:

- What could the boys **do**?
- What did they **find** in the schools?
- What was happening in **society**?
- What form did **elite levels** of sport take?

figure 8.6 – athleticism in the public schools

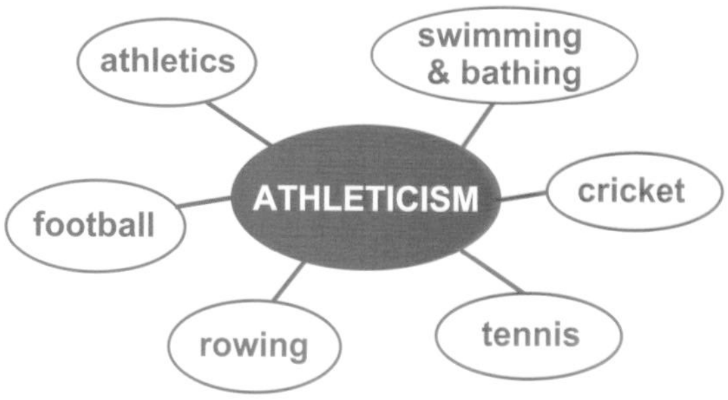

The six physical activities outlined in figure 8.6 were central sports in the public schools and are readily comparable with developments which occurred in society and at later dates. The term **athleticism** is a developmental term and the full expression of public school athleticism was not established until the 1860s. It had fundamental links with **Muscular Christianity** and reflected a philosophy of **physical endeavour** and **moral integrity**.

These values (physical endeavour and moral integrity) are at the heart of modern elite sport, though somewhat idealistic in the face of issues of deviance (cheating) and the doping culture.

Elite performance development

There were **three basic stages** or phases of development in these schools as discussed in the AS course, which allowed the high standard of sport and the expression of athleticism to flourish.

figure 8.7 – interschool cricket 1851

Phase one of development of sport in the 19th century public schools

Initially, the boys brought traditional ethnic sports into the schools, as part of their **free time** experience.

- **Mob games** were played which were dependent on existing facilities.
- **Contests** such as singlestick play and fighting were commonplace.
- The **rural hunting** experience was played out in hare and hound cross country runs.
- This is in addition to **cricket**, already widely enjoyed by the schools by 1850 (figure 8.7).

Phase two

Dr Thomas Arnold was the Head of Rugby School during the **second phase**:

- He was an **innovator**.
- He was the inventor of the **house** system.
- He actively encouraged **sixth form responsibility** and the **prefect** system.
- He was instrumental in the development of **compulsory games**.
- He was influential in linking **character building** values in and through sport.
- He had a love of **boating** and **bathing**.
- He was enthusiastic for his '**gymnastic gallows**'.
- He owned a house in the **Lake District**.
- While he was willing to flog boys, he was **prepared to listen** to their version of events.
- He felt that the unattended, un-timetabled, unescorted hours of a boy's day were as much a part of his education as the classroom itself.

What developed was the **right** for boys **to engage in sport**, and support from the Heads for **manly** activities as long as they were under the control of the prefects. From the boys themselves, there was a desire to be good at a **wide range of activities** so that they could represent their 'house' in competitions.

Phase three

During **phase three**, opportunities were extended and facilities built (figure 8.8) to encourage sports and games as a major educational and cultural vehicle.

figure 8.8 – public schools developed superb facilities

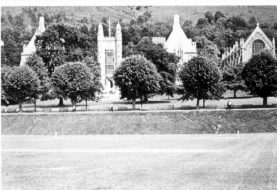

figure 8.8 – public schools developed superb facilities

Sports and games were seen to be:
* **Character building**, a major part of the popular religious cult of **Muscular Christianity**.
* Vehicles of **social control** with codes of **honour** and **loyalty** to the school and country.
* Dynamic **Christian values** presented sporting competition as a noble pursuit.
* Critics claimed that 'an ideal was turned into an idol' such was the extreme **status** given to the sports field.
* But sport has been the foundation stone of **amateurism**, so-called British **Democracy**, and **Modern Olympism**.

The **Clarendon Report** (1864) stressed the role of games in character building in the gentry schools and this was followed by the **Taunton Commission** (1868) which identified a large number of middle class boys' schools and Cheltenham Ladies College.

Boys leaving the public schools:
* Entered **Oxbridge** (the melting pot) and refined the rules of games.
* Achieved blues and carried **amateurism** and athleticism into society.
* Became **teachers** who were committed to athleticism as an educational vehicle.
* Formed **amateur governing bodies**, such as the FA, RFU, AAA and ASA.
* Extended **manliness** values abroad, encouraging **international amateur sport**.

Sport for girls and women

The evidence was that all these schools regarded **sport as an educational vehicle**, which encouraged talented boys and girls to **achieve excellence** in their chosen activity.

The spread of girls' high schools (figure 8.9) occurred some time later, which enabled these schools to develop their own brand of athleticism.

Within the processes of development undertaken by boys and men, **women** were largely **excluded**, and initially only the **sons of the gentry benefited**. However, the middle class schools were copying athleticism, and the sons of industrialists and businessmen took the enthusiasm for sporting excellence to the factories and the cities and eventually to the **skilled industrial workers** themselves.

figure 8.9 – cricket at an early girls' academy

STUDENT NOTE

Note that **women** were increasingly restricted by **Victorian attitudes** to their place in society.

Elite Sport

Elite levels of sport evolved because:
* School and even house teams displayed excellence.
* **Blues** were awarded to the best players at Oxbridge, many being outstanding players who played for **British** teams.
* The former pupils took **amateur games** to a level which rivalled the best professionals.
* Elite sport was organised for **gentleman amateur** sport initially, but eventually **changed the amateur code** to allow **working class males** to compete in organised sports at a high level.
* Former public schoolboys helped to organise and compete in the early **Modern Olympics**.
* The standard of coaching was such that Lyttelton and Foster were playing county cricket for Worcestershire while still at school, with several of their group going on to play for England.

The democratisation of sport in British society

As a product of public school graduates, rational sport was initially an exclusive development by the male upper and middle class and is normally described as the **Gentleman Amateur** period. Oxbridge sportsmen initially took the games to members of their own social group, forming games clubs and sports associations and eventually National and **International governing bodies**. These clubs and organisations were 'amateur' and **excluded the people** of the lower classes, who only had popular festivals and professional opportunities to participate in sport.

Exclusion

> **STUDENT NOTE**
>
> The crucial point concerning this '**amateur**' period was the element of purity of the morality of competition with others on an equal basis. This was to be unsullied by payment, wagering or corruption. Therefore participation had to be only by those who could afford to perform without payment, and who were the wealthy members of an upper or middle class in society.

The **FA** was formed by these gentlemen and the early soccer sides (like Sheffield) were all **gentlemen**. The FA Cup was won by old student clubs or urban gentlemen's clubs. Similarly, the early Athletic Clubs admitted **middle class gentlemen** who established and developed athletics and gymnastics.

These middle and upper class gentlemen were the new elite performers and the **lower classes and women were excluded**, leaving the prize fighters and pedestrians to make a living by competing in front of crowds and proving who was best. Opportunities for the lower classes and all women remained at an occasional festival level. Additionally, the lower classes needed to work for a living, and so had no **time** for this sort of thing.

Democratisation

During this period, there were political activists and religious reformers calling for improvements in the living and working conditions of the lower classes, and the sports movement existed within this wider reform process. The people running sport at this time promoted the notion that the **positive use** of 'free time' for the **workers** would **take them out of pubs** and allow them to play rational games, which had strong **physical** and **moral** values.

figure 8.10 – association football

Hence games and sport became **codified** and **regulated**, **regular**, **respectable** and **rational**, and the **numbers of people** participating expanded rapidly (figure 8.10, note the industrial city centre setting and the large number of spectators).

- The **Saturday half-day** and increasing **free time** (for factory workers) increased playing and training opportunities.
- The emergence of a **powerful middle class** together with a supportive commercial class.
- The '**early closing movement**' was achieved by shop assistants, with a subsequent development of **mid-week football** leagues.
- The **transport** revolution, particularly the growth of the **railways** from the 1850s, was closely linked with increased wealth and more free time.
- The **turn-pike system** improved roads and facilitated travel by carriage and stage for the wealthy. Eventually the bicycle (figure 8.11) allowed organised groups to cycle for sport and pleasure. There was also a second-hand trade in bikes.
- **Omnibuses** (buses) influenced the development of **suburbia** in very large towns.
- The **church** supported organised sport which was seen to have moral and health values. This was not only for the middle classes but also for commercial class youth, in the form of the YMCA and YWCA.
- **Benevolent** Quaker industrialists, Mechanics Institutes, Working Men's Clubs and Sunday schools promoted improved working class work conditions, **recreation and sport** (as well as education).

figure 8.11 – cycling in the 1890s

The notion of the **gentleman amateur** continued throughout the nineteenth century in some sports, but **Governing Bodies** gradually reformed their rules to change the class and gender **definition of amateurism** to a regulation based on **no financial gain**.

The professionals

Meanwhile, several games had acknowledged the place of the lower class **professional performer**, especially in cricket and association football. The professional player and club came under the **control of middle class administrators**, who accepted the code of physical endeavour and moral integrity as the basis of all modern games and sports.

Cricket engaged members of the lower class as groundsmen, but they were also chosen because of their ability as players and often fulfilled the role of **coaches** for gentry children. With games becoming **rationalised** and **regularised** in a society which was increasingly industrial and urban, the **standard of play** became important as a crowd attraction.

figure 8.12 – old-boys' association football

As a result, full-time professionals began to compete with the best amateurs (figure 8.12) and so were increasingly **paid according to their talent** and **crowd appeal**. But it was not until the 20th century that professionals were able to outplay the best amateurs and much later, with the ending of the **maximum wage** regulation (as late as 1961), that professionalism became attractive to the middle classes in most sports.

International developments

Cricket was the first sport to be taken by former **Oxbridge** students into the British Empire. This was the first sport to hold matches between national sides (USA v Canada, 1844). The main issues preventing such matches would have been the distances between the Empire countries and the cost of travel (it took 6 weeks to travel by boat to Australia for example) and of participating for the periods of time required to be spent overseas. Other sports (various forms of **football**, but notably **rugby** in Australia and New Zealand) followed. **Test matches** were the opportunity to 'test oneself against others', and this name became that used to describe **international fixtures** in these sports. The first official cricket test match between Australia and England took place in Australia in 1877.

The development of the Modern Olympics as an expression of excellence

By the 1880s, Britain had individual **Governing Bodies** in all the main sports with clubs and associations within their jurisdiction. They were **amateur** and mainly for **men** with some clubs retaining **exclusive** membership (this means that lower class men, women, and professionals at other sports were not allowed to compete). Alongside these were traditional games with traditional multi-sport programmes which were not recognised as amateur because they continued to accept professional athletes. Also there were **Athletic Sports occasions** in most towns and the main ones applied AAA and BCU rules.

Dr Penny Brookes had also established the **Much Wenlock Olympian Games** as a multi-sport event with amateur regulations (by the 1890s), but **international sport** as such was still very much in its **infancy**. England was involved in games of cricket with the larger Commonwealth (then **Empire**) countries. Individuals competed on the continent, particularly cycling in France and climbing and skiing in the Alps, but there was **no real need** for **International Governing Bodies**.

The place of Britain in the development of the Olympic games

Britain, therefore, had a major programme of wide-ranging amateur sports:
*   Promoted at the height of **public school athleticism** and copied by grammar schools.
*   Having individual **governing bodies** and national **competitions** in all the amateur sports and games.
*   Most open to **all classes**.
*   Emergence, after a delay, of **women's sports**, many with their own governing bodies.
*   Running parallel to **professional** soccer and rugby league.
*   With many of the **old remaining sports festivals** finding a place for **professional** athletes and cyclists.

The Olympic Games

Towards the end of this period (1876), **Baron Pierre de Coubertin** came to England to see the athleticism at Rugby School and the Much Wenlock Games. What he saw precipitated the dream of reviving an international Olympian movement, expressed through sports and high culture. His first step was to form an **International Olympic Committee** in 1894. Thirteen nations were present and 21 others wrote letters of support leading to the following resolution:

> 'In order to maintain and promote physical culture, and particularly to bring about friendly intercourse between the nations, sports competitions should be held every fourth year on the lines of the Greek Olympic Games and every nation should be invited to participate.'

The Modern Olympics

Hence, in 1896 the first **Modern Olympic Games** was held in **Athens**. Thirteen nations sent representatives, with many participants making it at their own expense. On the opening day there was a crowd of 80,000 including European Royalty. There were only nine sports:

- The 13 man **American** team dominated the athletics.
- A **Greek** shepherd showed great bravery in winning the marathon.
- A **Frenchman** won the 100 metres in white gloves.
- An American **swimmer** wouldn't swim because the water was **too cold**.
- An **English** tourist won the tennis.
- There were only **250 competitors** in all.
- The event had involved the **rebuilding of the original stadium**. Greece was lucky to find a philanthropist who footed the bill.

figure 8.13 – the first four modern Olympic Games

The **1900** Olympics in France (figure 8.13) was a virtual failure as far as sport was concerned as the French organisers focused on **cultural aspects**. The **1904** Games in St. Louis, America, was hardly a world event, with 432 American competitors out of 554, and **Americans winning most of the medals**. The whole Olympic occasion was dwarfed by a World Fair, which was held at the same time. The **1908** Games in London put the Olympic Games on the map, and this was paralleled in **1948**, when Britain agreed to hold the 'Victory Games' despite the devastation of World War Two.

20th century society needed to change and with it the status of the **amateur** and the **professional** sportsperson. This was the last vestige of sport as an exclusive club for the wealthy white male amateur athlete and coach.

20th century developments

- **Amateurism** increasingly became defined on a **financial** basis rather than social class status.
- The **Berlin Olympics** established a new problem for world games – the use of the world stage to promote politics and **nationalism**.
- The political problems of the **Cold War** became apparent at Helsinki (1952) and the Hungarian uprising at Melbourne (1956).
- Issues arising from **altitude training** and the '**Black Power**' demonstration in Mexico City (1968).
- **Terrorism** and the Munich Massacre (1972).
- **Political boycotts** at Montreal (1976), Moscow (1980) and Los Angeles (1984).
- The problems of increased **professionalism** among athletes.
- **Corruption** among IOC Commissioners in the 1980s.
- The **commercialisation** problems of the so-called 'hamburger' games in LA (1984) and the 'Coca Cola' games in Beijing (2008).
- The on-going problem of drug abuse.
- Additionally, there was the problem of **debt in cities** holding the games, until the age of global commercial television changed everything.
- From 1984 onwards, viewing times had to suit the **sponsors** and the huge American audience. This almost certainly led to Atlanta being selected for the Centenary Games in 1996 instead of Athens.

STUDENT NOTE

These developments were summarised in the book 'AS Revise PE for Edexcel, ISBN: 978 1 901424 54 6', pages 112 to 116.

21st century developments
- The main issue evolved from the **professionalisation** of all sport included in the Olympic Games from 1996.
- Most of the top Olympic competitors are now **full time** professionals making a living from their sport.
- Sportspeople obtain sponsorship, and advertise products (for a fee), on the basis of their global sports-star status.
- They are exposed to extensive media hype, which enhances their financial worth to a sponsor or commercial employer.
- Usain Bolt - global superstar - (figure 8.14) lives and trains in London for part of his year, undertakes visits to schools to promote sport, earns lots of money by competing in the Athletics Grands Prix circuit, and earns even more money by being present at commercial events.

figure 8.14 – Usain Bolt superstar

Post-war Europe and communist developments in East German sport

One other major post-war development acted as a major factor in present day sporting excellence. It was the **Cold War** between the USA and the USSR, where the **communist** regime chose sport as a '**shop window**', pouring money into sports schools, sports facilities and the promotion of advantages for talented performers.

This was done partly to appease the long suffering Soviet citizens, but also as a **propagandist** exercise to sell **communism** to the rest of the World as a **superior system** to that offered by the capitalist West.

The cold-war frontier battle was addressed by Soviet funding of **East German elite sport**. Though the quality of life for the average East German was extremely poor, **promising athletes** were given a **privileged lifestyle** within a sport's talent selection system.

In this system, young people were taken to **sports schools** (the second tier of the DDR sports pyramid, figure 8.15), with outstanding facilities and leading to **specialised university programmes**, with expert coaches and advanced facilities.

Potential East German Olympians, therefore, had this privileged lifestyle, with these support facilities, both physical and human. Perhaps because some of these '**advantages**' existed in **American universities** for sports graduates, it meant that this approach was accepted as '**study**' (and therefore '**amateur**') not **professionalism**.

figure 8.15 – the sport pyramid in the DDR

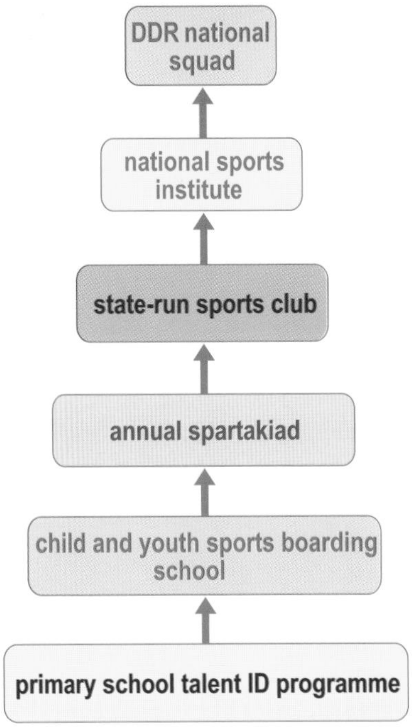

DDR national squad
↑
national sports institute
↑
state-run sports club
↑
annual spartakiad
↑
child and youth sports boarding school
↑
primary school talent ID programme

STUDENT NOTE

The development of the DDR sporting system was summarised in the book 'AS Revise PE for Edexcel, ISBN: 978 1 901424 54 6', pages 130 to 132.

East Germany, the Deutsche Demokratische Republik (DDR)
- **Scientific testing** and physical preparation went on to establish the **most suitable** **sport** for individuals.
- There were advanced **training techniques** and full-time training **opportunities**, with **full-time professional coaches**.
- There were special **diets**, which often included institutionally directed performance enhancing drugs.
- It was almost a cloning of the Soviet Union's own programme.
- It included **state sponsorship** of **workers sports clubs**, with **full-time** training opportunities.
- This disguised the first steps towards the large scale preparation of full-time athletes as a **political vehicle**.
- There were even Soviet-style **Spartakiads** (sports festivals sponsored by industry and workers' unions), giving performers competitive experience behind the 'Iron Curtain'.
- The 1960s marked the period when **anabolic steroids** were being systematically given to East German performers.

Sport in the DDR

- In the case of **East German female athletes** (figure 8.16), numerous world records were smashed. It has taken up to 20 years for most of these records to be broken by highly trained western athletes.
- The regime, allied to the German stoic mentality and situated as it was on the border to the West, was an ideal '**shop window**' – a window where the West could only see what was meant to be seen and the Berlin Wall kept the imbalance of life in East Germany concealed.

Methods of '**talent identification**' were very thorough, and huge sums of money were spent to support this small group of elite sportspeople for political ends. Unfortunately, institutional (political) pressure encouraged **illegal methods** to be used to achieve success.

figure 8.16 – Marita Koch - a product of the DDR system and still holder of the World record for the 400m sprint from 1985

> **STUDENT NOTE**
>
> Note that the DDR system was a centralised model, everything was decided and propagated by the state. This is in contrast to the USA system which is almost completely decentralised, with decisions made at local or college level depending on local spectatorism and funding.

Re-unification of Germany and the collapse of the Berlin Wall

The 'Cold War' was not a one-sided effort by the Soviet Union. The USA had poured money into West Germany to present a '**shop window**' into the East. The main result of the wall coming down was the realisation that East Germany was a bankrupt society with the exception of their success in Sport.

However, there was much to learn about East German success in sport, particularly in **coaching standards**. There was little else for the West Germans to gain, other than the sense of a united nation and the massive task of bringing the East up to the standard of the West. The fear was that there would be a massive migration to the affluent West, but this was forestalled by a major building policy in East Germany, where money and work were made available to encourage the population to lift themselves out of decay. Needless to say, the **sports facilities** and **expertise** in the East have not been wasted.

Since 1989 and the fall of the Berlin Wall, many countries have tried to copy the DDR system as an organisational structure, namely, Cuba, Australia, the UK, and China.

Australia, its sporting values and the AIS

With the emphasis on elite sport, Australia has established a system, some of it learnt from the East German experiment, but very much adapted to the sporting values and ambitions of Australian culture.

The obsession for sport in Australia

The focus of the teaching of sport and physical education in schools was on sport as a necessary experience for the development of a balanced, active and healthy lifestyle. This for some is the initial **opportunity** and **provision** for becoming a talented performer.

The dominant Australian lifestyle is far more actively linked with sport than in Britain. It is probably a myth to believe that all Australians are obsessed with sport, but a far greater proportion are physically active in sport and at least equally committed as spectators of urban professional sport. For these reasons, lifetime sport or life-long physical activity are identified as valuable goals in life, enabling people to live longer with fewer health complications and with a greater enjoyment of a full and active life.

Sport and the pursuit of excellence in Australia

- The mobilisation of Australia into a leading nation in World sport marks an amazing transition, changing from a sport loving society with a history of professional urban games, into a modern super power in terms of elite sports management and co-ordinated strategies for developing Olympic sports talent.

- After winning eight gold, seven silver and two bronze medals at the Munich Olympic Games in 1972, the Montreal Games of 1976 did not produce one Australian winner. In Britain, obesity among children alerted the government to the issue of **lack of general fitness** among the population. In Australia it was the Montreal failure which made the same point to the Australian government.

The master plan, the AIS and State sports institutes

* Unlike many countries, the Australians decided to do something about it. It was recognised that a pyramid structure of development was essential, and also that there needed to be a local - regional - national organisation to facilitate the progression from grassroots to excellence.

* There was clearly a need for better coaching, improved facilities, pre-games international competition and the freedom, both financial and in terms of providing the time for training, to train as hard as the Europeans. Here they really meant the East German model. The old philosophy 'to do your best' was no longer enough.

* By 1980, a master plan had been devised, but the boycott of the Moscow Olympics in that year became another issue. The Australian government was in favour of a boycott, but competitors voted to compete in the games under a storm of criticism and without displaying the Australian flag.

figure 8.17 – the AIS at Canberra

* The concept of the **Australian Institute of Sport (AIS)** was announced in 1980, to be based in Canberra (figure 8.17), with comments that it must serve the elite, but not miss out on the grass roots.
* In its first year, of 800 applicants 152 were successful. 72% came from the seaboard cities of Sydney, Melbourne and Brisbane with ages ranged from 13 to 30 in eight sports.
* It was decided that 15 hours a week must be spent on 'career training' – meaning studies away from the training environment which would provide qualifications for a future almost certainly not supported financially by sport.

In effect Britain has now adopted parallel programmes some twenty years later.

* Given the size of Australia, it was deemed necessary to establish a **second administrative tier** at State level.

* For example the **Victoria Institute of Sport** was established in Melbourne. Once these were established, it was agreed that there would also be a **decentralised** activity specialisation established in these State centres.

* For example, Melbourne was nominated as the National Tennis Centre (figure 8.18 shows the newly roofed centre court during the Australian Open of 2006).

figure 8.18 – Melbourne National Tennis centre

* A **third tier** was then established in the major towns in each State, where again certain sports were focused, but not to an extent where others were ignored.

* There remained the problem of distance given the size of the country, but this was overcome to some extent through **village facilities** being upgraded and **school programmes** being revised with also the provision of **residential facilities**.

Talent development

With an **administrative pyramid** established and **new facilities** to match, the Australians made sure that what they provided was backed up by **science** and exhaustive **research** of the latest American and European developments. The European influence was really that of the DDR, without the authoritarian and political conformity of that State. The developments included the latest **coaching methods**, so that programmes for sports teachers and high level coaches were established to produce the best from the sporting pool.

The final step was an awareness that the **early recognition of talent** had been the key to East German developments. **School programmes** were updated with various **competitive sports awards**, and a stringently applied **testing system** was used to identify young talent. This would lead on to early selection for State and/or national squads and top class coaching.

STUDENT NOTE

The **Sports Search programme** was set up to identify the physical characteristics of elite perfomers in different sports. Then the talented kids were channelled into a sport which suited their individual physical attributes. For example, tall long-limbed athletes might look at rowing, and short supple individuals might enter gymanstics or weight lifting.

Australian success

- Given the commitment of the Australian public to sport, this country has levels of success (figure 8.19) far outweighing the limited size of its population.
- Australia's natural competitiveness meant that some amateur values were off-set by a strong desire to win, but not to the extent that drug abuse would be any part of that.

- The **pyramid programme** is jointly focused on **active participation** in life-long sport and healthy exercise, with the intention of discovering talent and developing this into **World class performances**.
- The elite level of the pyramid identifies particularly with the Olympic Games, Paralympic Games, World Championships and Commonwealth Games.

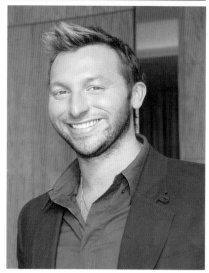

figure 8.19 – Ian Thorpe, multiple gold-medallist, is an Australian sports superstar

However, there is an older **traditional** system of selection, particularly in **major games**, which took amateur performance through to sponsored payment and into full professionalism. This system, dominated in the past by class distinction, has become a **pathway for the talented** to achieve considerable wealth as **professional** players.

A Case Study of the 'Super Roo' Bike

Australian **track cyclists** were World Track Champions for the three years from 1995-1997 and owed much of this to their **Super Roo carbon fibre cycle** (figure 8.20), built by a project team at the RMIT (Melbourne) and the advanced support programme of testing the machine and training cyclists at the AIS. This not only ensured a thorough scientific evaluation of cycle design, but the best riders in Australia were allowed to train on **personally adjusted** models for various international track and road events. In 1995 it won an Australian Award for Excellence from the Institute of Engineers, Australia. Designs were made for both track and road racing and its performance in both cases was outstanding from 1996 onwards. The chief designer was Sal Sansonetti, an Australian rider in the Montreal Olympics (1976) and his company brought the necessary racing expertise to the parent company.

figure 8.20 – Super Roo bike

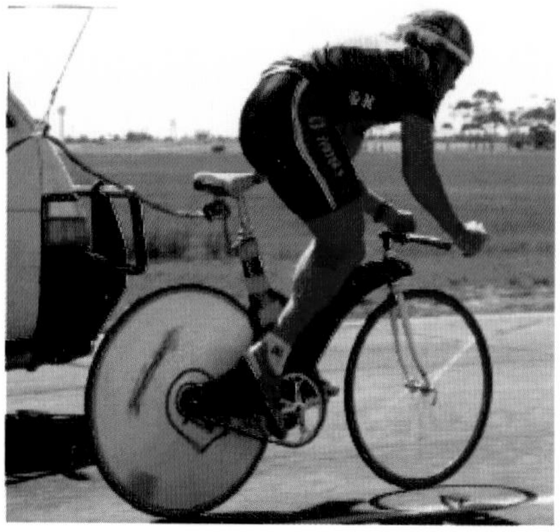

- The use of a **carbon fibre shell** produces a bike weighing around 5kg and allows the possibility of making an aerodynamic shape, without traditional handlebars, but giving the **maximum strength** with the minimum amount of material. Australia has the patent for this cycle, and makes various frames, but uses an Italian company to make and distribute parts.

- Nicknamed the **Superbike**, it took the World by storm in 1996 and with the high quality training available at the AIS, the Australians had the edge on the rest of the world, that is until other countries bought the bikes and subsequent models of it for their own riders. The cycle was not only lighter than any other, it had a superior personally adjusted aerodynamic design, tested in a **wind tunnel** at the AIS and using material already tested in space programmes.

- The superbikes were first available for riders in the 1994 Commonwealth and the 1996 Atlanta Olympic Games and produced winning riders in both. This success was not all limited to the Australian teams, since this was a highly profitable commercial enterprise. The company now makes purpose bikes for track, touring and mountain biking. Top cycling countries have invested in these cycles, and Britain has taken advantage of the new concept, resulting in **British victories** in the 2008 Beijing Olympics and the World Track Championships.

The place of elite sport in American society

School Sport in the USA

A percentage of American children of pre-school age have an opportunity to be taught fundamental sports skills through organised play in a programme called **Smart Sports Development**. This physical education approach is continued by qualified teachers in the elementary schools, where many classes are mixed, movement and dance are taught as well as games skills, and where enjoyment is more important than competition. This is similar to the UK.

Commercialisation of children's sport

However, it is the commercial development of children's sport which dominates the initial development of sporting values and opportunities and this lies outside the educational system and as such tends to reflect many of the values identified in professional sport in the USA. Children's sport is well-organised in the USA, with such titles as, **Pop Warner** and **Little League** Gridiron Football, **Biddy** Basketball and Little League Basketball. **Pee Wee** Baseball and **Little League** Baseball are both well-organised and available throughout middle class America. With the advent of **Title IX**, there was a marked increase in opportunities for girls. There is a strong role taken by **parents**, but evidence of a major competitive element can deter less able children.

Little League sports of **gridiron**, **baseball** and **basketball** all have characteristics of **elite sport**. While there are the elements of fun, safe practice and the development of sound attitudes, there is an under-swell of competitiveness coming from coaches and parents who want their kids to play hard and win trophies. This is the '**American Way**', perhaps even the '**American Dream**', where the personal ambition of individual parents to win a mini super-bowl is encouraged by the attention given to **competitive** sport by local **media** and **commercial** companies.

figure 8.21 – children's sport in time out

There is also a major policy to supply **sports facilities** and support **organisation** for youth sport, particularly for inner city youth. Though identified as lifetime sport, the **community** motive is to get trouble off the streets. Coaches and players make the games highly competitive, with individuals hoping to get the break into college with a **scholarship** and ultimately into the **professional** ranks.

The latest trend is to include a wide range of games, like soccer and softball, as well as the traditional baseball and basketball. This is controlled by the **National Alliance for Youth Sports**, with an initiative called **Time out for better Sports for Kids** (figure 8.21).

Sport ethic

The **three main ethics** promoted in American school sport and society are:

*   The **Lombardian Ethic**, which is the dominant sport ethic and supports the notion that **winning is everything**. This rejects the European and Olympic ideal that taking part is most significant and fair play an essential component. The Lombardian ethic almost totally controls the professional sports scene, and remains a central philosophy in most athletic departments in schools.

*   The **Radical Ethic** is nearer to the '**sport for all**' European view and is increasingly encouraged in the mass participation of sport. This is particularly so with the more recent encouragement of lifetime or '**lifelong**' sport strategies to encourage popular active involvement in sports. It is evident in school PE departments as educational values to counter the traditional Lombardian focus on achievement. The Radical Ethic encourages inter-mural school sport and the educational values of enjoyment, mass involvement in active sporting activity and fair play attitudes.

*   The **Counter-Culture Ethic** is the **opposite** to the Lombardian win ethic and is aligned with non-competitive physical recreations. In society it is often linked with the eco-sport movement, with the value of adventurous outdoor activities in the natural environment being emphasised. In the school system it is readily identifiable with the summer camp movement.

As in Britain, there was a period when educationists tried to **take competition out** of school life. Physical educationists in the UK promoted educational gymnastics and dance as non-competitive activities, particularly at primary school level. Today in both Britain and the USA, a **compromise** has been reached, where educationally based, non-competitive activities sit beside inter-mural sport.

The organisation of high school sport

The organisation of high school sport at District and State level is considerable. There is a national advisory body called the **State High School Athletics Association** (SHSAA) with branches in each State and this controls all **interscholastic** athletic (any sport) competition. Each State has its own **Inter-scholastic Association** which is financed by individual school athletic programmes. The sub-division of this is according to the size of the school, where there are five '**conferences**' from small schools of some 200 students to the largest schools with around 2000 students.

figure 8.22 – Phoenix Arizona High School football

- In most high schools there are **coaches** appointed for most of the high profile sports (figure 8.22).
- Market forces determine that the coaches' pay is normally higher than that of the teaching staff.
- This reflects the **status of that sport** in the school and community.
- In larger schools, there will be a **team of coaches** in the major sports.
- The coaches are all accountable to the Athletic Director of the school, whose aim is to exclusively **improve sport at the elite level**.

Unlike Britain, where spectators are attracted to professional games, American **inter-scholastic games** have a **major spectator base**, largely because the size of the country means that the 'local' team is the school team. Consequently, the inter-scholastic **sports facilities are excellent** and complete with major spectator seating and **media coverage**, giving the school a major source of revenue as well as community significance.

The high prestige of inter-scholastic sport holds a major place in the American psyche and influences:
- The **well-being** of the community.
- The place of **professional** sport in American society.
- The **media** which promotes sport.
- The **morale of the school** which is enhanced by sports success.
- The fact that **spectators and the community** are brought together as well as earning the school considerable revenue.
- The degree of commitment by the cheerleaders.

An example of the commercial impact of inter-scholastic sport is the school district in Colorado which sold the 'naming rights' to its new stadium for $2million.

University sport and inter-collegiate elite sport

Students graduate from their high school at the age of 17 with a high percentage going on to a two year Junior College programme, with approximately half of these continuing to degree programmes at universities, teachers' colleges and professional schools.

Given the high percentage of children who go on to college education, many young people have access to **outstanding sports facilities**. This is in a system of higher education where **sports scholarships** are available for the most talented and also as an **opportunity** for poorer members of society. The scholarship **regulations** are often **stringent**, demanding considerable commitment to train and play and with conditions of maintaining playing standards. Again, this approach is more **professional** than the normal British university sports club, which has to cater for all who apply for membership and is run on minimal funding.

The problem for these 'sports students' is that they have a harsh sport regime to follow and tend to pick 'soft' courses to study alongside their sports programme. This separates them from the student body and although they have huge support from committed spectators (which funds the whole sports programme in most colleges - similar to the high schools - see figure 8.23), the student body as a whole tends to question their academic commitment.

Students accept these conditions because:
- It is an accepted, even valued pathway through college.
- They have been striving for this since the little leagues.
- There is considerable parent enthusiasm and school kudos.
- Successful games players receive adoration from student fans.
- There is the chance of winning a college rose bowl.
- The '**pro-draft**' is a chance to earn a fortune playing professionally.

figure 8.23 – the University of Arkansas Razorbacks stadium

In statistical terms, the **NCAA** (National Collegiate Athletic Association) suggests that at least 20% of college gridiron and basketball players enter university on sports scholarships. This policy is sometimes called '**special admit**', suggesting that some of these candidates are allowed admission on lower grades. There is nothing unusual about this as it occurs regularly in English universities with centre of sports excellence status.

In addition to huge 'multi-universities' and State universities, the **Ivy League Colleges**, akin to Oxford and Cambridge Universities in the UK, not only offer the **largest scholarships** for the best high school players, but young people and parents are only too aware that sporting excellence can get their child into a top university with a scholarship to off-set the very high fees.

The quality of performance in specific high level games at college level, depends on producing **winning teams**. This, in itself, attracts large groups of spectators and sponsorship money, which in turn pays for high quality coaches and facilities. With the professional fixtures spread over a huge country, state colleges and universities become the spectator base for most games, leaving professional games to be supported on TV.

The pro-draft

This tradition not only gives collegiate sport a **high profile**, but provides major income as well as **recognition** as the final 'draft' into the **professional** ranks.

- The pro-draft gives the athletic departments considerable wealth and status. Athletic directors, **coaches** and trainers get **larger salaries** than many of the academic staff, because they command a major income from **spectators**, **commercial sponsorship** and **television** rights. If successful, the popularity and status of the institution is enhanced.

- The **pro-draft** is the process of selection of **top college players** in American football and basketball by the **professional major league clubs**.
- Once an athlete has completed a successful 4 years at college (university), he is ranked (by a panel from the colleges) according to ability and potential at his sport.
- This ranking is then accepted by the major professional teams, and the lowest ranked professional team has the **first option** at drafting the **best players**, with the top professional side having to accept lower ranked players (if any).

- The **pro-draft** is the apex of the **American sporting pyramid** set out in figure 8.24.

figure 8.24 – the sporting pyramid in the USA

numbers of males participating in the **big four** sports 1994

ELITE

PERFORMANCE

PARTICIPATION

FOUNDATION

BASIC

	numbers	%
professional	3,155	0.164
college	90,629	4.7
high school	1,919,080	100

the big four sports are - football, basketball, baseball, ice hockey.

The pro-draft

Most students in this system aspire to being **selected** to play for a professional club or a place in the national Olympic squad. Given the massive following for competitive sport in the USA, it is understandable why so many see the pro-draft as a gateway to higher education as well as a prosperous career. As with soccer in the UK, the drop-out rate is significant, but they do get an education that many English boys sacrifice for a possibly unsuccessful professional sports career.

The totals in figure 8.24 suggest that only 4.7% of high school players get scholarships and only 3.5% of these get onto the pro-draft (which is therefore 0.164% of high school players).

The American Dream

The term '**American Dream**' is expressed in American sport. This idea supports the notion that **anyone** from whatever background, especially the poor and ethnic minorities, can achieve **success** and **wealth** through hard work and talent. This ethic is often referred to as the **American Way of Life** (figure 8.25).

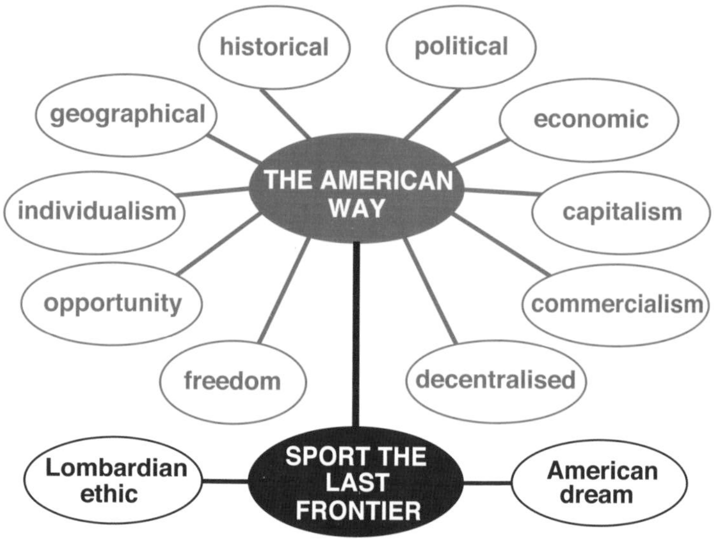

The '**American dream**' is a phrase which goes hand-in-hand with the slogans '**Land of the Free**' and the '**Pursuit of Happiness**', somewhat idealistic parts of the democratic notion: '**every American has the right to reach the top**'.

The **American dream** promotes a striving society, and sport is an example of that 'dream':
*   Successful sportspeople can have great commercial value as **role models** for young people.
*   As role models they enable the promotion of sports clothing and shoes or other lifestyle products.
*   This enables top performers to live a lavish and enviable lifestyle.
*   This links with the **win ethic** in leading the majority of citizens into becoming **spectators** after leaving college.

figure 8.25 – the American Dream, the context

historical · political · geographical · economic · individualism · THE AMERICAN WAY · capitalism · opportunity · commercialism · freedom · decentralised · Lombardian ethic · SPORT THE LAST FRONTIER · American dream

The **American Dream** is intended to help reinforce America's traditional value system, which is based on the **Protestant Work Ethic** and **individualism**, with such beliefs as:
*   **Working hard** to succeed in a competitive society.
*   Expectation that there will be **rewards for success**.
*   The need for widespread and **equal opportunity** to enable a chance for this success.
*   Founded on the notion of **self-help**, where those who fail have themselves to blame.
*   A hire and fire policy to weed out failures.
*   Economically **driven by capitalism** and the mighty dollar.
*   Politically reflecting a modern western democracy, striving for a **fair and equal society**.

figure 8.26 – Michael Phelps - multiple Olympic champion in an amateur sport - is part of the American Dream

The **last frontier** is one of those American ideas reflecting the struggle to establish society in the 18th and 19th centuries. American sport is termed the last frontier, which implies that it has a rugged competitive nature involving toughness, individual inspiration and teamwork. The elements of this idea are listed in figure 8.25.

Elite sport in the USA is largely commercial in nature. The college scholarship system, and superb university facilities, provide the basis for the winners in both professional and amateur sports (figure 8.26).

STUDENT NOTE

Note that the USA system is almost completely **decentralised**, with decisions made at local or college level depending on local spectatorism and funding. Sport enthusiasm is locally based and funded.

Support roles and funding of elite sport in the United Kingdom

The funding of physical activity

There are three types of funding of sport in the United Kingdom. These are **public**, **private** and **voluntary** (see pages 136 and 137 of AS Revise PE for Edexcel, ISBN: 978 1 901424 54 6).

Public funding
Public funding of sport in the UK has **two** sources:

figure 8.27 – lottery funding in the UK

* The **first** is the funding through the **normal taxation** process. At a national level this is allocated as part of the budget and normally involves government contributions to major projects, like the 2012 London Olympics. Also, **local authorities** contribute to their own projects, such as local sport and leisure centres and school facilities. These would be financed directly through the Council Tax, and through indirect sources such as the PFI (Private Finance Initiative).

* The **second** is the funding through the **National Lottery** (figure 8.27) which has five strands: Health, Education and the Environment (33.33%); **Sports (16.67%)**; Arts (16.67%); Heritage (16.67%); and Charities (16.67%). The sports strand encompasses the Sports Councils, Governing Bodies, SportscoachUK, and the Youth Sports Trust. The total for the **2005/2006** year was **£3.3 billion** for **sport**.

There is some overlap between the two areas, for example, the **National Lottery**, through the Youth Sport Trust, funds some sports activities in schools, which are mainly run and funded by **Local Authorities**.

Private funding
The large soccer and rugby clubs employ a substantial team of organisers, coaches and medical support staff, as well as the players, and this to a large extent is dependent on **private funding** by spectators who watch games. Most clubs with significant spectatorship also derive considerable income from **sales** of replica kit (including boots, shirts, shorts, socks, hats, training tops, tracksuits, gloves, and almost any personal item to be worn or sprayed on to the body). Commercial **sponsorship** from firms who want their name or logo on players' jerseys also provides income to professional sport.

This system allows free enterprise and reduces the use of public money where clubs have independent means.

Volunteer funding
Volunteer funding is mostly in terms of the voluntary and unpaid contributions made by coaches and organisers who work in private or self-funding clubs most evenings.

The voluntary sector often operates through the **Governing Bodies** of individual sports, which also receive funds from the Public Sector via the National Lottery. Evidence suggests that some 90% of our administrators and coaches are volunteers who are sometimes paid expenses by local clubs. This approach is at the heart of British sport and encourages enthusiasts to help, particularly in the community. The fact that this help is not always forthcoming means that potential talent is lost. Deprived areas often miss out. But the sector still provides the expertise and opportunity for some elite sport.

UKSport, the UK Sports council
UKSport is responsible for managing and distributing public investment and is a statutory distributor of funds raised by the National Lottery. This body is accountable to parliament through the **Department for Culture, Media and Sport** (http://www.culture.gov.uk) and its aim is to work in partnership to lead sport in the UK to world-class success. Its goals are given the title 'World Class Performance' which is aimed to meet the challenge of the London Olympiad.

The home countries of the United Kingdom are served by subdivisions of UK Sport, in effect the Home Country Sports Councils who distribute lottery funding to the grassroots of sport:
* **Sport England**.
* **Cyngor Chwaraeon Cymru**.
* **Sport Northern Ireland**.
* **Sport Scotland**.

World Class programme

The UKSI, the UK Sports Institute (specifically the **EIS**, the English Institute of Sport), is a talent development organisation in that it provides the facilities (the **multi-sport hubs**) and opportunities for talent to develop. The aim is to produce performers at the elite level of the sport development pyramid (figure 8.28, note that HRF is Health Recreation and Fitness), and who will therefore become part of the lottery funded **World Class Programme** (figure 8.29).

The WCP has three levels:

*   **World Class Talent** – helping the sportspeople whose talent has been identified to progress towards elite level.
*   **World Class Development** – helping talented sportspeople who are competent performers to achieve a competitive edge.
*   **World Class Podium** – supporting sportspeople who have medal potential. They should be standing on the medal podium at the next world or global games for their sport – but particularly at the London Olympic Games and Paralympic Games 2012.

The World Class Programme will then support sportspeople with various services ranging from the use of the hub facilities, the use of the medical support systems run by the EIS, and lifestyle funding (in place of a salary) for those elite athletes on the top level of the programme.

Also, the programme has put in place top quality support people such as strength and conditioning specialists, medical support teams, sports science specialists, and sport psychology experts. These people's jobs are to advise on most situations facing the aspiring performer.

The main point of this activity is to provide a worry-free environment for the elite sportsperson to train for up to 6 hours per day for 6 days of the week (allowing for some rest and recovery time!).

figure 8.28 – UK sport development pyramid

elite	national standard public recognition
performance	coaching & development done at club & regional levels
participation	increasing leisure options & HRF aware promoted via extra-curricular sport
foundation	learning basic skills, knowledge & understanding, often delivered in PE programmes in schools

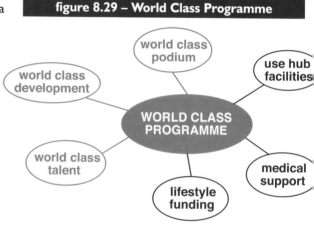

figure 8.29 – World Class Programme

Hubs and high performance centres

For the **elite amateur sportsperson**, these facilities have been the main recipients of the lottery funding process.

This was an approach developed by Sport England which aimed to combine community resources to create 'hubs' or multi-sport and activity centres. The aim was also to bring educational, social welfare and sports-medical services together under one roof.

Sports clubs are also encouraged to be part of the hubs, in order to identify and develop potential talent, and it is hoped that these multi-sport hubs will increase the level of participation in sport across England and the UK, as well as provide the superb environment required for the elite athlete.

There are nine **England regional hubs** operated and staffed by the EIS, plus one each in Cardiff, Edinburgh (the SIS headquarters are in Stirling), and Belfast.

The athletics hubs are at:
*   Loughborough University.
*   Birmingham Alexander Park.
*   Sport City in Manchester.
*   Gateshead.
*   North London Lee Valley.
*   West London Brunel and St Mary's Universities.
*   Bath University.
*   Sheffield Don Valley.

STUDENT NOTE

Note the LTAD (long-term athlete development) model summarised in the book 'AS Revise PE for Edexcel, ISBN: 978 1 901424 54 6', page 154.

As an example, the **Loughborough hub** has the following sports, plus EIS support including medical and physiotherapy and strength and conditioning facilities:

* Athletics.
* Triathlon.
* Swimming.
* Tennis.
* Cricket.
* Gymnastics.
* Women's soccer.

figure 8.30 – the Manchester velodrome

Hence the National Squads in all these sports are based at Loughborough, with facilities available for students, and squad members able to attend the university and continue studies.

Academies

The hubs provide the basis for academies, at which students can study, and train in ideal conditions with the best coaches. This is particularly the case at Loughborough, Brunel and St Mary's, and Bath Universities, who have hubs on site.

The same notion applies to 14-18 year-olds at **sports academies**. These are schools based in hub cities, in which designated elite performers are given time to train in the hub facilities (with the elite coaches) while pursuing an almost normal academic education. Some schools have boarding opportunities, so pupils who live outside the general area of a school can live and attend the school. An example of this is Burleigh College in Loughborough.

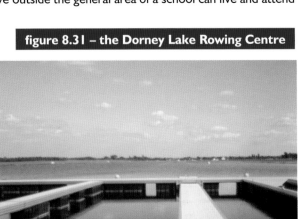
figure 8.31 – the Dorney Lake Rowing Centre

Most hub centres are based in university towns or cities, and hence students can utilise the facilities, though not quite so easily. But the hubs utilised by the governing bodies for National squads are more centralised. For example, the National cycling centre is at the velodrome in Manchester (figure 8.30). All members of the highly successful national cycling squad are required to live near the Manchester velodrome. This means that the conditioning, medical, and sports psychology backup teams are at hand as well as the coaching and training facilities.

The same is true of swimming and Loughborough University.

This is **not the same** as the **East German** system, but is a **British compromise** which works in the case of rowing, swimming and cycling particularly!

Note Dorney Lake Rowing Centre (figure 8.31), on the Thames near Eton, as an example of a privately owned world class rowing facility to be used for London 2012, and currently used by National squads.

The private sector

Other private sector academies are intended to support the elite development of various sports in the UK. This includes the Dubai International Sport City which includes tennis, soccer, golf, hockey and cricket options. Each option has excellent facilities, professional coaches, and highly organised and structured training, with an intensity appropriate to the academy philosophy. For a considerable fee!

Example of privately funded elite support in the UK

There is an excellent example of an advertising partnership in the case study of DIY Athletics.

This is a partnership between the **British Olympic Association** and **B&Q**. **Team B&Q** is an initiative where elite athletes are **employed** by their local B&Q branch on flexible hours which allows them to have time to train and also have time off for competitions. The Team B&Q includes eight current Olympic medallists, twelve aspiring Olympians and one potential Paralympian. B&Q is the largest specific employer of British sportspeople and has had a huge impact on the athletes concerned.

Team B&Q

These sportspeople have been virtually able to train full-time (figure 8.32). For example, British fencer, Jon Willis, is part of the programme and won the Heidenham Cup in 2007.

figure 8.32 – Sarah Ayton, Team B&Q - gold medallist, Athens 2004, sailing

Team B&Q has been running since the Athens Games in 2004. Community Outreach is an important part of the programme, where the team make regular appearances in-store and at community events. It is important to identify the generosity of B&Q in this venture, but also the advantages the company gains from it. The company is linked by association with the BOA (British Olympic Association), which is looking forward (in 2012) to its greatest moment since 1948.

The publicity value through these in-store appearances can have a massive influence on the public attitude as well as attracting people into the stores. Advertising alone puts the company in the public eye.

B&Q also supplied additional furniture and equipment (such as televisions, DVD players, rugs and irons) for the 280 athletes and support staff at the Beijing Olympics. To quote a B&Q marketing director, 'supporting the rising talent through the employment programme, as well as bringing the ideals of the Olympic Games to our staff and customers.'

This has been a partnership which has advantaged our athletes, but also a successful marketing ploy by the firm. Sadly, the recent recession led B&Q to withdraw its support in January 2009 (at the end of its then current contract).

This was a marketing strategy by B&Q and was bound to be less secure than the National Lottery. However, there have been advantages to both sides and as 2012 approaches, the international companies should start to compete to be sponsors, given the world-wide blanket coverage of commercial television during the games and leading up to the games.

Example elite programme: the Canadian carding system

The Canadian Carding System is a government scheme to financially assist promising, elite athletes. They are referred to as '**carded**' athletes and qualify if they are in the top 16 for their sport in world rankings. There is a government department, Sport Canada, which is responsible for this programme and recipients (figure 8.33) receive a monthly salary to meet training, competing and educational costs, but not total living expenses.

figure 8.33 – Brian Chibudu, Canada Cardist - long jump of 8.05m in 2009

It is the responsibility of individual governing bodies of sport to nominate these elite performers. This does not prevent individuals from receiving private sponsorship, but acts as valuable financial support as an incentive to strive for higher rankings. This State support is only part of a varied funding system.

For example, the Canadian 'carding' system:
*   Is only one element in the comprehensive programme of supporting 'State athletes', where in Canada individual freedoms are not denied and illegal drug use is being fought by Sport Canada and individual governing bodies.
*   If Australia identified talent selection as a number one priority, Canada has learnt about talent identification from Australia and is now focusing on a second phase, which is **elite athlete support**.
*   Because they are Commonwealth countries, they can usefully engage in '**borrowing**' strategies, because of their common heritage.
*   Canada and Australia are large countries with small populations, and therefore need to use government sponsorship as part of their financial strategy.

Sporting excellence

Sporting Excellence is the objective of most countries these days and advanced, industrialised countries like the UK, Australia and USA would be looking for a very **broad pyramid of opportunity**, in which provision for all and self-esteem for all minorities to participate are essential. To achieve these targets, **disproportionate funding** for sport is necessary for Olympic success. This is in a world which values sport highly as a barometer of the political and economic success of a country. The international standards of performance are so high that disproportionate funding has become a **fundamental necessity**. In all cases, the process can only be achieved through a pyramid process of getting promising performers to the top. The shape of that pyramid depends on the extent to which elitism is operating and funding is given.

Extrinsic and intrinsic values tend to lead to a balance between a professional administrative standard and required levels of sportsmanship. Each of the **five levels** of participation, the **activity**, **governing bodies**, the **performer**, the **administrator**, the **official**, and the **spectator**, need to be fully '**professionalised**' to establish excellence. The implication is that the broad base made up of spectators is going to have to pay a lot of money to fulfil this aim. Television, particularly commercial television, will provide a major part of elite sport income, along with commercial sponsorship of individuals and teams as in the USA.

Summary

STUDENT NOTE

Here we have a summary of the information needed to act as a basis for question analysis linked with recent developments in the United Kingdom and which has been largely covered, in the book 'AS Revise PE for Edexcel, 978 1 901424 54 6', Section 1.2 Performance Pathways – Talent, page 130 onwards.

The hints for a challenging A2 level question should be from:
* Awareness of the history lying behind the programme for elite sport in Britain.
* Case studies of different Olympic Games compared with Beijing.
* Changes in the opportunities for minority groups.
* Socio-cultural factors influencing the development of elite sport in the UK.
* Influence of the East German, Australian and Canadian approaches and the issue of successful cross-cultural borrowing.
* Lessons which have been learnt from America, particularly at collegiate level.
* The significance of the 2012 Olympic Games in the UK – profit or loss potential.

Practice questions

History and the development of Elite Sport

1) Explain the extent to which Pedestrianism acted as a pathway to social opportunity and financial wealth in the early 19th century in Britain.   4 marks

2) Discuss the extent to which pugilism reflected Regency culture.   6 marks

3) Describe the limitations which existed in the early Modern Olympics.   6 marks

4) Why were Oxford and Cambridge able to make such an impressive contribution to elite sport in the late 19th century Britain?   8 marks

5) Discuss the development of Saturday Half-Day and the emergence of working class sport.   9 marks

Elite Sport and the East German System

1) What were the **main** characteristics of the East German sports system?   4 marks

2) How did the Berlin Wall make East Germany a 'shop window'?   4 marks

3) Discuss the strength and weaknesses of the East German sports system. Why have so many countries adopted elements of the DDR system?   10 marks

4) Explain why there might have been problems when Australia adopted parts of the East German sports system and discuss Australia's policy.   8 marks

Elite sport in Australia

1) How is physical education in the Australian State of Victoria influenced by its size, its population density and its desire to promote elite sport?   6 marks

2) Use the example of the 'Super Roo bike' to explain progress made in elite sport and its connection with the Australian Institute of Sport (AIS). Discuss the justification of improved equipment on competition.   8 marks

3) Discuss the impact of Australia on elite sport in the United Kingdom and the problems associated with trying to incorporate elements of a different country's system into our own.   8 marks

Elite Sport and the United States

1) Suggest reasons why the USA were so successful in the early Modern Olympic Games.   4 marks

2) How did the American view of amateurism differ from that of the UK in the late 19th century and why was this the case?   4 marks

3) Explain the differences between sport in American schools and colleges, and sport in the UK school/college system.   6 marks

4) Why does the USA have so much success in Olympic Sport despite having a largely spectator based society?   8 marks

5) Outline some lessons which have been learnt from America, particularly at collegiate level.   20 marks

Elite Sport and developments in the United Kingdom

1) Describe the administrative system (institutes of sport) underpinning elite sport in the UK and account for its structure.   6 marks

2) How has the Team B&Q programme in the UK attempted to establish a balance between the needs of the BOA and commercial sponsorship?   6 marks

3) Briefly identify and describe what you think UKSport is doing to satisfy the needs of elite British performers. Why has Australia been able to help in this process?   8 marks

4) Discuss the policy of elite sport funding adopted by the United Kingdom.   8 marks

5) Explain the significance of the 2012 Olympic Games in the UK – profit or loss potential.   12 marks

6) In recent times there have been many changes in the opportunities for minority groups to participate in elite sport. The participation in physical activity and achievement of sporting excellence by young people have always been affected by social class status, personal financial circumstances, ability to travel, having the time to participate, gender, disability status, ethnicity and age.
   Outline the factors and issues which would affect participation for **two** of these groups in the UK.   20 marks

CHAPTER 9: *Technical support*

The sport science back-up required by the elite sportsperson lies within the areas of physiology, sport psychology, and biomechanics, and this book sets out in some detail above how the study of physiology and sport psychology helps sportspeople.

Biomechanics is the study of how forces are applied to the human body, or applied to objects associated with the human body, or applied by the human body in a sporting situation.

The role of technology in training analysis

Technology provides the tools for analysis of technique which would enable a coach to change patterns of movement of the human body, which would enable the body to exert or use force more efficiently. Efficiency of technique is the process where a movement is performed more fluently, with less energy expenditure, with less risk of injury or trauma, enabling the body to exert greater forces where necessary.

From chapter 7 above:
- Learning a successful technique is a **long-term process**, starting from basic skills specific to a sport or athletic event, then making adjustments as the perfomer learns how to perform.
- This is a complex matter because a young performer will **observe** others and will attempt to **imitate** them whether or not the technique being observed is correct.
- This depends on the **status of the role model** (whose technique is being copied), and the **complexity of the task**.
- Most young people will arrive at their first training session for a popular sport with some idea of the skill of the sport.
- Coaches like to start from scratch when it comes to teaching technique. This is rarely possible.

Refinement of technique involves:
- Knowledge of the **perfect technical mode**l by a coach.
- Knowledge of the **mechanics** of a skill.
- Being aware of methods by which technique can be **changed**.
- Being aware of whether a skill is gross or fine, and how this affects its learning.

Motion analysis

Motion analysis is that produced by **Quintic** (figure 9.1) or **Dartfish**, in which slow motion video is examined for body and limb angles, and then compared with a 'perfect' technical model.

Since technique is often an individual matter (depending on the stature and strength of the performer, for example), it would not always be the case that a performer would change his or her technique to mirror that of the model. The coach would have to be clear about the purpose of various features of the technique, and how this fits into its biomechanics before changes should be made.

Sports science

Sports science includes the services outlined in figure 9.2 which are provided to sportspeople whose aim is to analyse performance to suggest ways of improving that performance.

Performance measures are identified and recorded across these various disciplines. These measures then act as a benchmark for ensuring performance impact.

figure 9.1 – biomechanical motion analysis

figure 9.2 – sport science components

Sports institutes

There are four sports institutes in the UK:
*   English institute for sport (EIS), http://www.eis2win.co.uk/pages/
*   Scottish institute for sport (SIS), http://www.sisport.com/sisport/CCC_FirstPage.jsp
*   Sports Institute Northern Ireland (SINI), http://www.sini.co.uk/
*   Welsh institute for sport (Athrofa Chwaraeon Cymru, ACC), http://www.welsh-institute-sport.co.uk/

The main role of these agencies is to provide elite sports services to elite members of sports national squads.

These services are given across all sports, based on the elite multisport hubs spread around the UK (see page 102 above, and example, figure 9.3). There are 9 hubs in England, and one each in Wales, Scotland and Northern Ireland with the aim:
'a network of sport science and sports medical support services designed to foster the talents of our elite athletes.'

Elite athletes therefore have local access (from the high performance centres) to expert support services:
*   Sports medicine.
*   Physiotherapy.
*   Soft tissue therapy.
*   Nutrition.
*   Psychology.
*   Biomechanics.
*   Performance analysis.
*   Talent identification.
*   Strength and conditioning (figure 9.4).
*   Performance lifestyle.

figure 9.3 – the elite 50m pool at the Loughborough university hub

figure 9.4 – the powerbase strength and conditioning centre at Loughborough University

Case study, the Carnegie Centre for Sports Performance and Well-being

The Carnegie Centre for Sports Performance and Well-being opened in 2008 and is part of Leeds Metropolitan University. In addition to offering 'state of the art' training facilities, such as outdoor synthetic track, astroturf playing surfaces, gymnasia and conditioning fitness suites, its aim is to offer Sports Science Services, that are currently available at more favoured locations such as Loughborough, Brunel-St Mary's, Birmingham and Lee Valley. The idea is to attract more elite athletes as well as serving the public.

figure 9.5 – gymnastics at Carnegie, note the indices taped to the athlete, and the calibration boards behind

The university is a **TASS** (Talented Athlete Scholarship Scheme) hub institution which entails servicing talented athletes throughout the region and has high performance centre status for the following sports:
*   Netball.
*   Tennis.
*   Badminton.
*   Cricket.
*   Table Tennis.
*   Gymnastics, figure 9.5.
*   Weight Lifting.
*   Rugby League.
*   Hockey.
*   Triathlon.

The High Performance **Triathlon Centre** (figure 9.6) is currently the base for all the triathletes in the North of England who are on World Class Programmes. Currently there are 9 athletes aged between 14 and 20 who are supported by the centre and who either attend regular sessions at the University or who participate in monthly training camps held throughout the region. Elite athletes, such as triathletes, are offered '**Individual Support Programmes**' so that all specific facets of performance are analysed and each athlete is provided with individualised training advice and support athletes to increase performance and prevent injury.

figure 9.6 – triathlon at Carnegie

- **High Performance Centres**, such as the Carnegie Centre Facilities, include a large treatment room with dedicated physiotherapists and sports masseurs to provide support to injured athletes, and service sports performers during training and recovery.

- **Biomechanical** technical or **motion analysis** using the latest camera-computer link-up (figure 9.5), is used in sports in which technique is important.

- For example, performers can improve their lifting techniques, receive immediate feedback and take away video footage of their performance. Treadmill analysis gives feedback on key points of the body so that exact positions, such as hips, shoulders and knees can be highlighted graphically. $\dot{V}O_{2max}$ and other physiological testing on the treadmill can also take place (figure 9.7).

figure 9.7 – a dedicated physiology lab

- Technologies such as **Prozone** provide technical and tactical feedback for team sports (see page 80 above).

- The use of **force plate technology** provides information about the pattern of force made by a foot striking the plate (see page 81 above). A podiatrist works with the elite performer to assess any mechanical problems and to recommend appropriate orthotic aids that would correct foot motion issues such as excessive pronation. Allied with a 3D scanner this technology can be used in the construction of personalised footwear.

- Data from **wind tunnel technology** provides feedback to change/adjust the design of the aerodynamics elements of sports equipment and gives feedback such as optimal riding postures (refer to page 82 above).

- These scientific technologies are linked to undergraduate and postgraduate study and so benefit both elite performers and academic departments.

- The **body scanner** and '**body pod**' (a more favoured method because there is no radiation risk) offer the most accurate method of calculating body composition. Scanners can also be used to check for possible stress fractures that can result from highly repetitive training programmes.

- EVH (Eucapnic Voluntary Hyperpnea, a procedure requiring deep breathing under stress) **physiological testing** (figure 9.7) is used to analyse breathing and provides certification for asthma users required to satisfy International Governing bodies such as the IAAF.

- The Carnegie complex boasts an **extreme environment centre** which allows simulation of a variety of conditions which athletes might have to face, such as hot and humid conditions and altitude training for endurance-based athletes. Ice baths are used to reduce joint and muscle inflammation following intensive training (refer to page 47 above).

- **Sports psychology** and the best nutritional advice are two more facets of high performance centres. Sports psychologists are used to develop the mental preparation for both training and competition (refer to page 31 above) and help athletes deal with problems such as injury and preparing for lifestyle choices towards the end of their sporting careers.

- **Sports nutritionists** give advice on choosing the right food and fluid intake, adjusting diets for competitions, such as marathon races and triathlons, and nutritional advice important when recovering from intense training sessions (refer to pages 18 and 19 above).

Dedicated high performance sports centres - the Carnegie Centre

*   **Sports vision specialists** develop training programmes to improve visual acuity, hand-eye co-ordination, perception, reaction time and so on (see page 73 above).

*   **Professional coaches** employed by the EIS, governing bodies and universities, offer specific coaching services.

*   Like many centres of this type, Britain's elite athletes know there is a lot more to sports performance than practising their chosen discipline and have a number of centres to choose from.

Role of national agencies

The centralised model

One of the earliest countries to develop centralised sporting programmes for their elite athletes with high quality coaching and science and technical support was the former DDR. For a small country, the people of East Germany achieved some remarkable results (not all due to this structural model!!) in many sports including cycling, weightlifting, swimming, track and field, boxing, skating and other winter sports. One reason for the success was the leadership of Dr. Manfred Hoeppner which started in the late 1960s. This centralised model has provided a template for coaching development in other countries such as Cuba and Australia and Great Britain, and is expanded on page 93 onwards.

The decentralised model

In this model no single agency takes control, however there is development through pathways such as higher education institutions. The American Scholarship system is an example of this model. Refer to pages 98 above.
Sporting Academies are also part of this model, see page 103 above.

The UK's mixed system

Some sports in the UK adopt the centralised system with one or two centres in the UK for that sport (for example, cycling in Manchester, and swimming at Loughborough). The governing body organises the coaching and technical elements, and the EIS service providers work in close consultation with the national governing body of the sport and performance directors, coaches, and the athletes themselves. They also provide support to athletes not only on home soil but also when they travel to overseas camps and competitions at the request of the national governing body. Sports with a wider base (such as athletics) use a wider hub-based model, each hub having the EIS support as outlined above.

Sports supported include:
*   All summer Olympic sports with the exception of tennis and men's football.
*   All Paralympic sports.
*   A limited number of Winter Olympic and English sports.

The majority of the athletes we support are those who are UK Sport Lottery funded. The EIS (and other Institutes) are grant funded through the UKSport Lottery Fund.

Practice questions

1) Describe some existing English hubs/academies and their administration. Compare this with elements of the East German and Canadian systems.   16 marks

2) Describe how private academies can contribute to elite sport in the UK.   4 marks

3) Discuss the role of National Agencies in the development of an elite performer.   8 marks

4) The UK World Class Programme, that supports elite athletes, relies on the services of the three main areas of sport science, namely physiology, sport psychology, and biomechanics. How can an elite athlete use these services to improve his or her sporting performance?   12 marks

INDEX